EVERY LIFE
—— IS A ——
PLAN
OF GOD

Discovery House Publishers

Books, music and videos that feed the soul with the Word of God

Box 3566 Grand Rapids, MI 49501

EVERY LIFE
—— IS A ——
PLAN
OF GOD

Discovering His Will
For Your Life

J. Oswald Sanders

Unless otherwise indicated, Scripture is taken from the
HOLY BIBLE, NEW INTERNATIONAL VERSION.
Copyright © 1973, 1978, 1984 International Bible Society.
Used by permission of Zondervan Bible Publishers.

Library of Congress Cataloging-in-Publication Data

Sanders, J. Oswald, 1902—
   Every life is a plan of God: discovering his will for your life/
J. Oswald Sanders.
        p. cm.
   Includes bibliographical references.

   ISBN 0-929239-54-7

   1. God—Will. 2. Christian life—1960– I. Title
BV4501.2.S176 1992
248.4—dc20   92–26434
                                                        CIP

Discovery House Publishers is affiliated with Radio Bible Class,
Grand Rapids, Michigan

Discovery House Books are distributed to the trade exclusively by
Barbour Publishing Inc., Uhrichsville, OH 44683

Printed in the United States of America

08 09 10 11 / CHG / 11 10 9 8 7

Contents

Preface

I thought I had written my last book! But I have been urged from several quarters to write on the subject of guidance, in which there is so much interest and yet considerable confusion. So I have taken up my pen again.

It is now eighty years since as a lad I received Christ as my Savior. It is His grace and patience that have kept me on track. The succeeding years of Christian work around the world have afforded abundant opportunity to put into practice the principles I have incorporated in this slim volume and to prove their validity.

The subject is complex, and on some points one can be only tentative. As a preacher and missionary, I have naturally slanted my treatment of the subject in that direction, but the principles are equally applicable to those whose sphere is business, education, the farm, or the home.

I trust that the Holy Spirit may shed some rays of light on the path of those who read this multitude of words.

J. Oswald Sanders
Auckland, New Zealand, 1992

1. A Planned Life

Key Topics:
- Every Life Is a Plan of God
- The Element of Mystery
- Guidance Is Needed
- Does God Really Guide?
- Myths about God and Guidance
- The Will of God
- Does God Have an Individual Will?

> Go to God Himself, and ask for the calling of God; for as certainly as He has a plan or calling for you, He will somehow guide you into it. . . . By His hidden union with God, or intercourse with Him we get a wisdom or insight deeper than we know ourselves; a sympathy, a oneness with the Divine will and love. We go into the very plan of God for us, and are led along in it by Him, consenting, cooperating, answering to Him, and working out with the nicest exactness that good end for which His unseen counsel girded us and sent us into the world. In this manner we can never be greatly at a loss to find our way into God's counsel and plan.
>
> —*Horace Bushnell*

Every Life Is A Plan of God

One of the selections in the volume, *The World's Greatest Sermons,* was first delivered by the outstanding American preacher Horace Bushnell. It bears the title, "Every Life a Plan of God." This scriptural concept has met with wide acceptance among evangelical Christians the world around. In recent years, however, it has come under challenge, probably because of the unfortunate way the subject has sometimes been presented. Does God have an ideal and detailed will and plan for every life? Is this a valid concept, or is it only a view that has been read into Scripture wrongly. If there is such a plan, it is of paramount importance that we get to know it. If it is only a myth, the sooner it is laid to rest the better.

Everywhere in this beautiful world in which we live, there is evidence of a God who is working to a plan, vast beyond human comprehension. And yet when Jesus was instructing His disciples, He made this astounding statement: "Are not two sparrows sold for a penny? Yet *not one of them will fall to the ground apart from the will of your Father. . . .* So don't be afraid; you are worth more than many sparrows" (Matt. 10:29–31, italics added).

On another occasion He computed the worth of a single human soul in these terms: "What good is it for a man *to gain the whole world,* yet forfeit his soul?" (Mark 8:36, italics added).

If our majestic God includes even the insignificant sparrow in His overarching plan and beneficent will, and if the soul of man exceeds in value all that this world can offer, is it unreasonable to conclude that He has an individual plan and purpose for each human life? Each of us is the expression of a unique divine idea, and our purpose in life should be to cooperate with our Father in the outworking of that idea. Each of us is unique because we are made in the image of God. "So God created man in his own image, in the image of God he created him; male and female he created them" (Gen. 1:27).

If there is a divine plan for our lives, and I believe there is, we should not expect it to be like an architect's blueprint. Or like a travel agent's itinerary, all complete with dates, places, and times. We are not automatons controlled by a heavenly computer! Divine guidance concerns people who have been endowed with the awesome power of free choice. Every day we have to make decisions and choices, some of which will affect our whole future. The fact that we have been created in the divine image adds an eternal dimension to these decisions.

> Behind the scenes where we cannot see,
> A hand divine works the things that be,
> And brings to my path the scheme devised
> By the Maker of earth who built the skies,
> *But He leaves me to choose the life He plans,*
> Or to walk the way of self's demands,
> To build on the rock or the sinking sands.
>
> (italics added)

The circumstances surrounding our lives are not accidental but are devised by an all-wise and loving Father, who knows how best we can glorify Him and yet at the same time achieve our own highest good. When this becomes a conviction, believed and accepted, then every part of life becomes significant, and life itself becomes one long voyage of discovery of God and of our own true selves.

Divine guidance is neither mechanical nor automatic, for God does not treat us as robots but as intelligent beings. When He guides, He does so in such a way as to lead us into a wholesome maturity and a growing likeness to Christ. The whole guidance process is calculated to increase our knowledge of God Himself, not only of His will. "... everyone undergoes discipline.... God disciplines us for our good, *that we may share in his holiness*" (Heb. 12:8, 10, italics added).

Here is what the Lord undertakes to do:

> This is what the Lord says—
> your Redeemer, the Holy One of Israel:

> "I am the Lord your God, who teaches you
> what is best for you,
> *who directs you in the way you should go.*"
> *Isaiah 48:17* (italics added)

Our heavenly Guide does not deal with us *en masse,* but has personal and individual transactions with each. Since each of us is unique, He employs as many methods as there are people. In describing the particularity of the Father's care for His children, Jesus used a striking figure of speech: "Even the very hairs of your head are all numbered" (Matt. 10:30). This gives us assurance that no detail of heredity, no peculiarity of temperament, no handicap in environment escapes His compassionate eye. With infinite wisdom and sympathetic understanding He plans for us in love.

> This is what the Lord says: *". . . I know the plans
> I have for you,"* declares the Lord, "plans to
> prosper you and not to harm you, plans to give
> you hope and a future."
> *Jeremiah 29:10–11* (italics added)

God Does Not Desire Facsimiles

Many young Christians—and some older ones too—are inclined to entertain vain regrets that they are not like someone else whose gifts and personality they envy. It is one thing to admire and emulate the fine qualities of another, but to try to model oneself on him or her is a virtual denial that there is an individual plan of God for one's life. God's purpose is not to turn out facsimiles, but to develop and mature the unique personality of each of His children. He wants you to be you, not someone else—but a much better you, of course.

A chequer board of light and shade?
And we the pieces deftly laid?
Moved and removed without a word to say
By the same hand that board and pieces made?

No pieces we in any fateful game,
Nor free to shift on Destiny the blame,
Each soul doth tend its own immortal flame,
Fans it to heaven, or smothers it in shame.

—John Oxenham

As we seek God's plan for our lives, it is by no means uncommon to meet many obstacles in our way. But we must remember that God is training us for eternity. These obstructions are not necessarily an indication that we are out of His will, but are put in place to develop our faith and strengthen our character. It was so with Arthur Davidson, a student in the Bible College of New Zealand during my era there as principal.

The Unknown Plan

"Do you think it might be the Lord's plan for you to take the Bible College course?" a friend asked him. Arthur had not considered this possibility before, so he obtained the literature of the college.

"One serious problem confronted me as I considered the brochure," he wrote. "The course was designed chiefly for those called to missionary service. At that time I had neither the calling nor the physique necessary for overseas missionary service. Furthermore, such a training course would mean my taking a step into the unknown, for completion of the course did not assure a sphere of service after graduation. Such a prospect rather frightened me, after the security of several years of employment.

"That night, browsing through some material on my desk, I came across a poem entitled, 'The Unknown Plan.' It was based on Abraham's call to an unknown land, not knowing where he was going. As I read it, the words impressed me in such a way that I knew it was God's direction to me to take the unknown path and apply to the Bible College.

"Next morning, while I was filling in the application form, the doorbell rang, and I was greeted by a salesman whom I had met previously. When I told him about my plans, he answered, 'Brother, you'll make a great mistake if you take the Bible College course. Many ministers feel the training is most inadequate. I would strongly advise you to settle on another course of training.'

"It was a most disconcerting experience. Had I mistaken the message of the previous evening?

"Within minutes of the salesman's departure, my friend Jack, who had made the suggestion that I take the Bible College course, came in.

"I told him of my experience with the salesman a few minutes earlier, and he quickly interjected: 'Don't worry! That fellow was dismissed by the college for improper behavior when he was a student! The devil has tried to use him to turn you aside from the Lord's plan.' It was a timely and reassuring word to me, and I completed the application.

"Later that day I received another blow. The local doctor to whom I went for the required medical test, after examining me, startled me by saying, 'I'm sorry, but I can't pass you for such a course. Physically you are run down. My advice to you is to rethink your plans.' His blunt remarks left me reeling.

"Finally I decided to send the application papers with a brief note appended about my tiredness, and suggesting that I take the medical test after a holiday I planned. Later, when I took the test, I was given a clean bill of health."[1]

Arthur subsequently served with distinction for many years as the Australian director of a large mission. This should be an encouragement to others who meet lions in their path as they move forward in the direction they believe to be God's will for their lives.

> I am not strong, I am not wise,
> And many a path before me lies
> > Where I might go astray;
> So when I have to make a choice,
> Help me to listen for your voice,
> > And then obey.

The Element of Mystery

When Moses was delivering his farewell message to the nation of Israel, he made this pregnant statement:

> The secret things belong to the Lord our God, but
> the things revealed belong to us and to our
> children forever, that we may follow all the words
> of this law.
> > *Deuteronomy 29:29*

This verse enshrines both encouragement and warning. Encouragement, because it assures us that our God has revealed in the Scriptures everything necessary to enable us to live godly and joyous lives. Warning, lest we become presumptuous and arrogantly intrude into areas that are peculiarly God's and that He has not been pleased to reveal.

We are finite creatures and, as such, should not expect to comprehend every facet of the wisdom of the infinite Creator God who instructed us:

> "My thoughts are not your thoughts,
> neither are your ways my ways. . . .

As the heavens are higher than the earth,
so are my ways higher than your ways
and my thoughts than your thoughts."

Isaiah 55:8–9

Since this is so, should we be surprised when at times we find ourselves baffled and mystified by God's dealings with us and in the world? There are "secret things" that belong to God alone, and we will have to wait until eternity dawns for their explanation.

When Jesus was preparing His disciples for His impending departure, He forewarned them that they would be mystified and would even stumble because of some of the experiences that lay ahead. But He promised that at the appropriate time—His time—they would be able to understand the meaning of those experiences. Here are His words: "You do not realize now what I am doing, but *later you will understand*" (John 13:7, italics added). God does not always explain Himself. He loves to be trusted.

At a time when I was facing an important decision, I came across this pungent paragraph from the pen of Samuel Chadwick, the great Methodist preacher. It had a special message for me.

> We are moved by the act of God;
> Omniscience holds no conference;
> Infinite authority leaves no room for compromise;
> Eternal love offers no explanations;
> The Lord disturbs us at will;
> Human arrangements are ignored;
> Business claims put aside.
> We are never asked if it is convenient.

So we can expect that sometimes we may have to be content to await the future explanation of the mystery of God's dealings.

When God called Abraham at seventy-five years of age to leave his comfortable home in Ur of the Chaldees and embark on the life of a nomad, he "obeyed and went, even though he did not know where he was going" (Heb. 11:8). It is characteristic of faith that it is willing to step out under sealed orders.

During World War II, when travel by sea was a precarious business because of the prevalence of submarines and mines, our ship was zigzagging in its course. I asked the captain the reason. He said that in the interests of safety he was traveling under sealed orders. He was just following the course plotted by his superiors in whose wisdom and experience he had complete confidence. Sometimes our Guide asks us to travel under sealed orders, just trusting His love and wisdom.

Carey's Fire

William Carey and his colleagues in Serampore, India, faced as devastating a mystery as anyone could imagine. A fire ravaged the buildings that housed their printing presses, destroying ten years of translation work on the Scriptures. Dictionaries, grammars, and manuscripts in several languages, which no money could buy, compiled laboriously and at great cost, went up in flames. How could the sovereign Lord allow such a thing to happen? Mystery indeed!

What were the reactions of those affected by the tragedy? They experienced the blessedness of which Jesus spoke to the disciples of John the Baptist when He said, "Blessed is he who takes no offense at me" (Matt. 11:6 RSV).

Carey's first sermon after the fire had as its text, "Be still, and know that I am God" (Ps. 46:10). It had two points:
1. It is God's right to dispose of us as He chooses.
2. It is man's duty to acquiesce in His will.

Marshman, his colleague, referred to the calamity as "another leaf of the ways of Providence, calling for the exercise of faith in Him whose word, firm as the pillars of heaven, has decreed that 'All things work together for good to them that love God, to them who are the called according to his purpose' (Rom. 8:28 KJV). Therefore be strong in the Lord."

The tragedy turned into triumph. Fuller, who was Carey's friend and representative in Britain, wrote to him:

> The fire has given your undertaking a celebrity which nothing else, it seems, could, a celebrity that makes me tremble. . . . The promptitude with which you have been able to repair the loss of your types and renew your printing of the Scriptures is as extraordinary as if we had repaired your pecuniary loss in a week.[2]

> All is of God that is, and is to be;
> And God is good! Let that suffice us still;
> Resting in childlike trust upon his will,
> Who moves to his great ends,
> Unthwarted by the ill.
> —*J. G. Whittier*

Guidance is Needed

It is a common illusion that man is competent to direct his own life, to be master of his own destiny. Every day the marvels of science and human ingenuity leave us breathless, but unfortunately the advancement of science has not been matched by the progress of morality. The horrors of the Gulf War that is raging as I write are not convincing proof of man's ability to control his fate either individual or corporate. Innumerable ruined lives bear mute but eloquent witness to unaided man's inability to shape his own destiny.

Writing by inspiration, the prophet Jeremiah presented the divine estimate of man's competence: "I know, O Lord, that a man's life is not his own; *it is not for man to direct his steps. . . .* The heart is deceitful above all things and *beyond cure.* Who can understand it?" (Jer. 10:23; 17:9, italics added).

The wise man adds his exhortation: "Trust in the Lord with all your heart and *lean not on your own understanding"* (Prov. 3:5, italics added).

"The shrewdest calculations and the keenest insight can never be adequate for our supreme need, nor be a substitute for the knowledge of the divine mind." For the Christian, daily guidance is an indispensable necessity. But experience teaches that not everyone who professes to be seeking the plan of God for his life is sincerely committed to doing God's will if it is revealed.

An architect once complained that many of his clients who asked him to design a house for them would subsequently reveal that they had already designed it for themselves. What they really wanted from him was his sanction of the home they had planned and the addition of the necessary professional architectural touches.

In a somewhat similar fashion, many Christians go to the great architect of lives, not so much to discover and accept His plan as to seek His approval of their own. They are really seeking consent, not guidance and direction.

More than human wisdom is required if we are to reach correct decisions in the complex situations and relationships of today's world. Our own wisdom is too limited, and our long vision too defective.

There is another limiting factor. The disposition of events is not in our hands, but in God's. Often we find ourselves in circumstances over which we have no control. We can neither forecast the actions of others nor regulate them. In one hour the whole complexion of life may be changed—bereavement, ill health, layoffs, collapse of the stock market can change the whole picture. In these days of worldwide economic recession, many now enjoying an affluent lifestyle may be suddenly reduced to poverty. *The only certainties and realities are the spiritual and the divine,* so we are cast back on God.

> I faced a future all unknown,
>   No opening could I see;
> I heard without the night wind moan
>   The days were dark to me—
> I cannot face it all alone!
>   O be Thou near to me!

In realistic and strangely contemporary language, the apostle James envisaged a situation such as many are facing today. "Now listen, you who say, 'Today or tomorrow we will go to this or that city, spend a year there, carry on business and make money.' Why, you do not even know what will happen tomorrow" (James 4:13–14).

We are not immune to "the slings and arrows of outrageous fortune" simply because we are Christians. The same rain falls on the just and the unjust. The fact that God eulogized Job as "a blameless and upright" man, did not exempt him from the trauma of seeing his whole world collapse around his ears. But because his confidence in the faithfulness and love of God never wavered throughout the whole drama, he emerged from the tragedy enriched and not impoverished.

In addition, we are faced with a massive upsurge of demonic forces, concerning which all too many Christians are woefully illiterate. As we draw nearer to the end of the age, we can expect to see the fulfillment of Revelation 12:12: "Woe to the earth and the sea, because the devil has gone down to you! He is filled with fury, because he knows that his time is short." We do not need to look far to see that fulfillment.

A recent news article carried this paragraph:

> A wave of fascination with the occult is noticeable throughout the country. It first became apparent a few years ago in the astrology boom. But today it extends all the way from Satanism and witchcraft to the edges of science. . . . Major publishers have issued dozens of hardcover books on the occult and the related field of para-psychology in the past year. . . . A growing number of colleges across the U.S. are offering courses on aspects of the occult.

We need a wisdom and power infinitely greater than our own to tread safely through the mine fields that our wily adversary has sown all around us. But God be thanked, we have a Guide who has safely traversed them all, and has promised to lead us through them, too.

> Not for a single day
> Can I discern the way;
>   But this I surely know,
> Who gives the day
> Will show the way,
>   And so I surely go.
> —*John Oxenham*

Does God Really Guide?

One of the sure signs of advancing spiritual maturity is an increasing desire to know God and, after that, to come to know His will for one's life. This was evident in the experience of the apostle Paul. Once he had met the risen

Lord on the Damascus road and was convinced that Jesus was indeed the Son of God and Lord of all, his immediate reaction was to ask, "What shall I do, Lord?" (Acts 22:10), knowing full well that the answer would turn his life upside down. Henceforth it was his passion and delight to be Christ's willing bondslave. He expected to receive guidance, and he was not disappointed.

When Dr. E. Stanley Jones, eminent missionary to India, was asked the question, "Does God really guide?" he replied, "It would be strange if He didn't! He who made the tongue and gave us the power to communicate with one another, shall He not speak and communicate with us?"[3]

Would it not be strange if the One whom Jesus taught us to call "Father" did not extend detailed guidance to His children who came to Him asking for it? The implication is inherent in the very idea of fatherhood. Those of us who are fathers know how delighted we are if our children come to us when perplexed and how glad we are to give guidance.

From among many Scripture passages that supply an answer to the question, here are some representative ones:

> I will instruct you and teach you in the way that
> you should go; I will counsel you and watch over
> you. (Psalm 32:8)

> For this God is our God for ever and ever; he will
> be our guide even to the end. (Psalm 48:14)

> The Lord will guide you always; he will satisfy
> your needs in a sun-scorched land. (Isaiah 58:11)

> Good and upright is the Lord. . . . He guides the
> humble in what is right and teaches them his way.
> (Psalm 25:8–9)

When an Alpine climber wishes to scale an unfamiliar mountain, he engages the services of an experienced and competent guide. Once engaged, the guide assumes responsibility for the success and safety of the mountaineer. Even so, the ultimate responsibility for guidance rests on the One who undertakes to be our Guide.

It is the shepherd who is responsible for leading and protecting the sheep, not the sheep themselves. Left to their own devices, sheep become hopelessly lost and open to attacks by predators. Their part is to be sensitive and responsive to the shepherd's call, and then to follow where he leads.

This is the very example Jesus used to illustrate the relationship that exists between Him and those He calls "my sheep": "I am the good shepherd. The good shepherd lays down his life for the sheep" (John 10:11). "The sheep listen to his voice. He calls His own sheep by name and leads them out. . . . his sheep follow him because they know his voice" (John 10:3–4).

What Kind of Guide Is He?

Moses had a great longing to know God more intimately—to know His "ways" so that he could conform to them. In other words, he wanted God's guidance in the deeper things of life. So he prayed, "If you are pleased with me, *teach me your ways*" (Ex. 33:13, italics added). How eagerly God responded to his plea! "And the Lord said to Moses, 'I will do the very thing you have asked' " (33:17). No reluctance on God's part.

This emboldened Moses to ask for something even more wonderful: "Now *show me your glory!*" (33:18, italics added). God answered just as readily as before, but in an unexpected way. He did not turn on a pyrotechnic display but did do something that Moses never forgot. *God revealed His essential character to him,* for God's glory is His character.

> Then the Lord came down in the cloud and stood
> there with him and proclaimed his name, the Lord
> . . . the Lord, the compassionate and gracious
> God, slow to anger, abounding in love and
> faithfulness, maintaining love to thousands, and
> forgiving wickedness, rebellion and sin. Yet he
> does not leave the guilty unpunished.
>
> *Exodus 34:5–7*

This is the kind of God we have for a Guide! Yet too often He is misrepresented and misconceived as a kind of ascetic ogre, a celestial killjoy who delights in denying His children what they desire when they come to Him for guidance.

In his classic, *The Knowledge of the Holy,* A.W. Tozer underlined the importance of a correct conception of God and the peril of false ideas of Him.

> A right conception of God is basic, not only
> to systematic theology, but to practical living as
> well. . . . I believe there is scarcely an error in
> doctrine or a failure in applying Christian ethics
> that cannot be traced finally to imperfect and
> ignoble thoughts of God.[4]

Although in the fullest sense God is incomprehensible, He has graciously condescended to reveal Himself (in part) in terms we can comprehend—in the created universe, in His holy Word, and supremely in the person and work of His Son.

1. *In the Created Universe*
> The heavens declare the glory of God; the skies
> proclaim the work of His hands. Psalm 19:1

> The great Jehovah, enthroned in His glory,
> Controls the rolling orbs of space;
> And world to world is proclaiming the story
> Of power divine, and matchless grace.
> The earth lofty is veiling His splendour,
> The sea a myriad song will raise,
> The sky so lofty is veiling His splendour,
> Creation all resounds His praise.

2. *In The Scriptures*

God has given a fuller revelation of Himself in His Word, which records in comprehensible form all we need to know about His nature and being. It may not be, certainly will not be, all we would *like* to know, but it is all we *need* to know to enable us to lead holy and joyous lives. Further, He has sent His Spirit who inspired the Scriptures, to "guide [us] into all truth" (John 16:13).

> The heavens declare Thy glory, Lord,
> In every star Thy wisdom shines,
> But when our eyes behold Thy Word,
> We read Thy name in fairer lines.
> *—Isaac Watts*

3. *In the Person of His Son*

The supreme revelation of God is in the person of His Son, who made the astounding claim, "Anyone who has seen me has seen the Father" (John 14:9). If we desperately want to know what God is like, all we have to do is to look at Jesus. He is the perfect revelation of God's character and the perfect model for our emulation.

Because this is so, any supposed guidance that does not fit the revealed character and teaching of Christ is immediately suspect and should be discontinued. Josiah Conder expressed this truth in noble words:

In Thee most perfectly expressed,
The Father's glories shine;
Of the full deity possessed,
Eternally divine.
Worthy O Lamb of God art Thou,
That every knee to Thee should bow.

With this reassuring picture of our heavenly Guide we are in a position to lay to rest nine myths that reflect adversely on Him.

Myths About God and Guidance

The foregoing conception of God, our heavenly Guide, is not the picture entertained by all who come to Him for guidance in life's decisions. There are many myths and misconceptions of our God, held even by sincere, Bible-believing people, who have somehow absorbed Satan's subtle aspersions on His love and goodness. During World War II, I was rather shocked when a mature Christian lady said to me, "I wonder if after all God is really as good as we have thought Him to be?"

Here are some of the unfounded myths that should be laid to rest permanently:

1. *That if we surrender our wills to God He will ask us to do some difficult thing we don't want to do.* It is true that God does sometimes ask people to do difficult things, but only if He sees that, *in the long run,* it will prove to have been in their highest interests—and He knows what these are better than we do.

2. *That God will ask us to do something irrational by normal standards.* On the contrary, the God who created rational thought will never ask us to act irrationally. Because His thoughts are infinitely higher than our thoughts, on rare occasions He may ask someone to do something that may be

beyond reason (as we know it), but nothing that is contrary to reason.

3. *That if there is something we want to do desperately, the likelihood is that God won't want us to do it.* But God has made it abundantly clear that He will gladly fulfill our right desires, on one condition:

> *Delight yourself in the Lord;*
> And He will give you the desires of your heart.
> Commit your way to the Lord,
> Trust also in Him, and He will do it.
>   *Psalm 37:4–5 (NASB,* italics added)

If we delight ourselves in Him and His interests, if like Paul "we make it our goal to please him" (2 Cor. 5:9), our desires will increasingly become one with His. The only desires the Lord wants to frustrate are those He sees will harm and not help us. Let us settle it in our minds once and for all that God is not an ascetic who delights in saying No!

4. *That if we make a faulty decision and miss God's will, we are doomed to a second-best life thereafter.* I knew a great man of God who was greatly used into his nineties. During one period he was head of a Bible college, and during his tenure there, one thousand young men and women were trained and entered upon Christian work, many of whom are still serving around the world. However, he had made an unhappy and unfortunate marriage, as a result of which his purpose of going to the mission field was frustrated. In speaking to his students, he sometimes said that because of that, he was experiencing only God's second best. But was he correct in saying that? We can never choose the second best from God. He gives no second bests.

Paul assures us that the will of God is "good, pleasing and perfect" (Rom. 12:2). That means that it can't be improved on. "Every good and perfect gift is from above, coming down from the Father of the heavenly lights, who does not change" (James 1:17). Guidance is a gift from God, it cannot be earned.

It is, however, possible for us to refuse His gift of guidance, make a costly mistake, and yet later ask for and receive forgiveness (1 John 1:8) and return to Him for guidance. Does God give us only second best then?

The parable of the potter and the clay gives the answer (Jer. 18:1–5). When the vessel the potter was shaping was "marred in his hands," presumably because of some lack of malleability in the clay, did he throw it away on the scrap-heap? To the prophet's amazement, he took the very same lump of clay—doubtless after remedying the defect—and "formed it into another pot." Did he make one that was second best? Indeed no!—"shaping it *as seemed best* to him" (italics added). The Lord said to recalcitrant Israel, ". . . can I not do with you as this potter does?" (18:6). God never does anything second best!

> Marred in the making, but with wondrous patience
>   Takes He the clay
> Into His hands, and fashions slowly
>   In His own way.
> Just what I was the world can only see—
>   He looks beyond and sees what I can be.

To the penitent soul, God's present will for him or her is never second best, irrespective of past failure. Where by repentance, confession, and renewed surrender, past sin and failure are "washed in the blood," it is never too late to make a new beginning. Once again it is possible to prove afresh "what God's will is—His good, pleasing and perfect will" (Rom. 12:2).

5. *That the normal and adequate mode of guidance is through impressions made on mind and heart by the Holy Spirit* with appropriate accompanying feelings. This is dealt with more fully in chapter 3.

6. *That our intuitions are the direct voice of God.* There is no scriptural basis for this contention. In any case, our intuitions are no more reliable than the relevant information we have gleaned.

7. *That every open door or favorable concurrence of circumstances constitutes a call from God* and is a sufficient warrant to move forward. Of course it may be so, but remember that Jonah found favorable circumstances—an open door into the inside of the great fish! It would be wise to check by other criteria, too.

8. *That a closed door is the end of the matter.* Again, it may be so, but it may be that only the front door is closed. There may be an open back door or window. This has often proved to be the case. One mission serving in the southern Sudan was expelled by the government, but its workers did not cease praying that the door might reopen. Ten years later they were invited back by the very same government that ousted them! So keep on knocking.

> Is there some door closed by the Father's hand
>> Which opened you hoped to see?
> Trust God and wait—for when He shuts the door
>> He keeps the key.
> Have patience with your God—your patient God
>> All-wise, all-knowing, no long tarrier He,
> And of the door to all the future life
>> He holds the key.

William Carey had an embarrassing experience with a closed door, which, none the less, ended happily. God had long been preparing him for work in India. In 1793, accompanied by his friend Wood, he tried to sail there, but the East India Company was so jealous of its rights in the country and so fearful of anything that might interfere with its trading that it would not allow any missionaries to land on its territory. Therefore, before Wood and Carey had even gotten out of the harbor, they were sent ashore again.

They were naturally terribly disappointed. Had they mistaken God's guidance? Were all their years of toil and travail in vain? It looked like it. They went into a restaurant to have a meal. A waiter handed them a slip of paper that gave the address of a Danish shipping company, to which they hurried. To their delight they found that there was a ship due to arrive soon that could take them to their destination.

Divine providence was behind the disappointment. Previously, Mrs. Carey had been unwilling to accompany her husband to India, but during the time of delay, she was persuaded to go with him, taking their children as well.[5]

We must not interpret every delay or seemingly closed door as the end of the matter. The Lord says, "I am he that shuts and no man opens, and opens and no man shuts" (Revelation 3:7).

9. *That we receive guidance from God by making our minds blank*, and taking the thoughts that surface as God's guidance. This practice was popularized many years ago by Frank Buchman, founder of the Oxford Group Movement (now Moral Rearmament). This runs exactly counter to the teaching of Scripture. Jesus made it painfully clear that more than the voice of God can be heard in the human heart. "Out of the heart come evil thoughts, murder, adultery, sexual immorality, theft, false testimony, slander" (Matt. 15:19). And, as J. I. Packer has said, "Those who assume that whatever 'vision' fills the blank is from God, have no defense

against the invasion of obsessive, grandiose, self-serving imaginations spawned by their own conceit."[6]

In counseling the Colossian Christians, Paul did not advise them to make their minds blank. Instead he told them he prayed that God would fill them "with the *knowledge* of his will through all spiritual *wisdom* and *understanding* (Col. 1:9, italics added). This is only one of many passages that indicate that in guidance, and indeed in all Christian living, the intellect is not to be bypassed, but is to be used to the utmost under the control of the Holy Spirit.

The Will of God

Thou sweet, beloved will of God,
    My anchor ground, my fortress hill,
My spirit's silent, fair abode,
    In Thee I hide me and am still.

O will, that willest good alone,
    Lead Thou the way, Thou guidest best,
A little child, I follow on,
    And, trusting, lean upon Thy breast.

Thy beautiful sweet will, my God,
    Holds fast in its sublime embrace
My captive will, a gladsome bird,
    Prisoned in such a realm of grace.

Upon God's will I lay me down
    As child upon its mother's breast;
No silken couch, nor softest bed,
    Could ever give me such deep rest.

Thy wonderful grand will, my God,
    With triumph now I make it mine;
And faith shall cry a joyous Yes
    To every dear command of Thine.
                —*Gerhardt Tersteegen*

The Will of God

> Be transformed by the renewing of your mind.
> Then you will be able to test and approve what
> God's will is—his good, pleasing and perfect will
> *Romans 12:2* (italics added)

That sounds very attractive and reassuring! But not everyone, Christians included, would use the words "good, pleasing and perfect" to describe his or her concept and impressions of the will of God.

The Oxford English Dictionary defines the will as "the mental faculty by which a person decides upon and controls his own actions or those of others." My will is what I plan and purpose; God's will is what He plans and purposes. Paul speaks of "the purpose of his will" (Eph. 1:11).

As a result of the fall of Adam and Eve in Eden, man's will is set on a collision course with God's will. The independent exercise of the human will appears early in a child, even in a baby. The little daughter of a friend of mine once said to him, "Daddy, I do like to do what I do like to do!" Unconsciously, she was expressing the universal tendency of humankind.

We love to do "our own thing," even though at times it is the exact opposite of the will of God. The prophet Isaiah described this fatal tendency hundreds of years ago, and there has been no essential improvement in human behavior since then. "We all, like sheep, have gone astray, each of us has turned to his own way" (Isa. 53:6).

How different was the will of the Last Adam during His life on earth. He set a noble example that we are to follow. "Your attitude should be the same as that of Christ Jesus" (Phil. 2:5). Here is the model:

> When Christ came into the world, he said:
> "Sacrifice and offering you did not desire, but a

body you prepared for me; with burnt offerings and sin offerings you were not pleased. Then I said, 'Here I am—it is written about me in the scroll—*I have come to do your will, O God.'* "

Hebrews 10:5–7 (italics added)

As His life drew to a close, His agonized prayer in the Garden of Gethsemane revealed how true He had been to His pledge: "My Father, if it is possible, may this cup be taken from me. *Yet not as I will, but as you will"* (Matt. 26:39, italics added)

We often pray as the Lord taught His disciples—and us— "Your will be done on earth as it is in heaven." We long for it to be done not only in the world, but in our own hearts as well. Yet many who pray that prayer regularly have a jaundiced view of God's will. They tend to associate it with the undesirable and painful experiences of life. To them it is the antithesis of "good, pleasing and perfect."

Aspects of God's Will

In defining differing aspects of the divine will, writers and preachers use different terms. Some distinguish between the *directive* will of God, what He ordains, and the permissive will of God, what He allows. This commonly accepted view is often supported by citing Israel's demand of Samuel that it be given a king like the other nations (1 Sam. 8:6–9). In speaking with Samuel, God rightly interpreted this demand as the rejection not of Samuel, but of Himself and His rule. What was His response? "Listen to them; but warn them solemnly and let them know what the king who will reign over them will do," was His command to Samuel. God did not ordain it, but He permitted it.

However, this view creates a serious problem, which is treated helpfully by A. Morgan Derham in his book *The Mature Christian.* I venture to quote him at length:

What does it really mean when we say He *permits* but does not *send* something? Are we not in fact saying that *He chooses not to intervene?* We dare not say that He *cannot* intervene if He wants to.

The whole Bible is against that idea. If a child asks a parent, "May I do this?" and the parent replies, "I won't stop you," is the parent's responsibility any less than if he had said, "Yes, do it by all means"? Just a little, but not enough to excuse him if something goes seriously wrong.

Ultimately we have to come to the point which the Apostle Paul reached in Romans 9:19–21: "One of you will say to me: 'Then why does God still blame us? For who resists his will?' But who are you, O man, to talk back to God? 'Shall what is formed say to him who formed it, "Why did you make me like this?"' Does not the potter have the right to make out of the same lump of clay some pottery for noble purposes and some for common use?" To this question, Scripture gives a satisfying answer. To some of our unanswered questions, we will have to fall back on Abraham's affirmative question: "Shall not the Judge of all the earth do right?"[7]

The Cross of Calvary is the sufficient answer. "The cross assures us of God's intention. Creation assures us of the sufficiency of His wisdom and skill."

Others speak of the *general* and the *particular* will of God. There are some things that are for all humankind and other things that are His will for only a particular nation, group, or individual—and that extends to the details of daily life.

Still others differentiate between God's *sovereign* will—a predetermined plan for everything that happens in the universe—and His *moral* will—His revealed commands in the Bible that teach us how we ought to believe and behave. Added to those is the *individual* will of God, God's detailed life-plan for the individual.

This last aspect has been challenged by some who can see no such thing in Scripture. They contend that if in our decision-making we keep within the sovereign will and the moral will of God, there remains a wide range of options for the individual for which guidance is not required. Personal matters can be decided satisfactorily by claiming and exercising the wisdom promised in James 1:5. But is there an individual will and plan of God for each life?

Does God Have an Individual Will?

In the previous section, reference was made to the view that God has a sovereign will and a moral will, but that He does not have an individual will for each person. Proponents of this position would argue that most Scriptures that seem to teach that God does have an individual will can be better understood as descriptive of God's moral will.

In the limited space available, let us consider two such passages. In writing to the Ephesian Christians to establish the truth that while good works can never merit salvation, they are the inevitable outcome of genuine faith, Paul penned these words, "For we are God's workmanship, created in Christ Jesus to do good works, which God prepared in advance for us to do" (Eph. 2:10).

In his commentary on this verse, Francis Foulkes had this to say:

> "This does not *of necessity* mean that there are particular good works that are God's purpose for us. *There can be no objection to such a concept if it is reckoned that the foreknowledge of an*

almighty and omniscient God is not opposed to His gift of freewill to men" (italics added).[8]

Bishop Handley Moule adds this thought:

> The phrase [which God prepared in advance for us to do] does not state but clearly implies that Divine pre-arrangement so maps out, as it were, the duties and the sufferings of the saint that his truest wisdom and deepest peace is to "do the next thing" in the daily path, in the persuasion that it is part of a consistent plan.[9]

So while the primary purpose of this verse is not to demonstrate that every life is a plan of God, the verse is quite consistent with that view.

Another passage that is consistent with God having an individual will is Psalm 32:8–9:

> I will instruct you and teach you in the way you
> should go;
> I will counsel you and watch over you.
> Do not be like the horse or the mule, which have
> no understanding
> but must be controlled by bit and bridle or they
> will not come to you.

Opinion is divided as to the identity of the speaker of this portion of the psalm. Psalm 32 is obviously connected with Psalm 51, for both refer to David's sin with Bathsheba. Because of this connection it has been suggested that David is the speaker of verses 8–9, and that these two verses are part of his response to his pledge in 51:13: "then I will teach transgressors your ways."

This interpretation is faintly possible, but it requires considerable ingenuity to imagine in what way David could fulfill the fourfold undertakings of the verses:

"I will instruct you."
"I will teach you."
"I will counsel you."
"I will watch over you."

In his *Favourite Psalms,* John Stott sees God as the speaker of Psalm 32:8–9,

> David's expression of confidence in God in v. 7 is immediately answered by God's promise of personal guidance, for in His steadfast love He is concerned not only to forgive the past but also to direct the future. . . . But God's guidance is not intended to save us the bother of using our own intelligence."[10]

Indeed, the four promises of the speaker are so general and all-embracing that they could be discharged rightly only by God. Some see in these verses a picture of a mother teaching her child to walk, with her eye constantly on him. That surely is very personal and individual guidance.

There is a salutary lesson for us to learn from verse 9, for this passage is at once a promise of guidance and a warning against obstinacy and insensitivity where the guidance of God is concerned.

Opinion is divided as to whether this passage can rightly be regarded as teaching that God has an individual plan for every life. Gary Friesen concludes: "Even if God is viewed as the speaker, He is seen teaching His way of righteousness.

This customary usage fits the context, so an individual will of God is not in view."[11]

Is this a necessary deduction? It does fit the context, but does it exhaust the verse? Does God's way of righteousness not include the details of daily life in which God has so clearly expressed His interest?

It is generally accepted that the King James Version rendering, "I will guide thee with mine eye," is not an accurate translation. The New International Version's "I will counsel you and *watch over you*" and the Revised Standard's "I will counsel you *with my eye upon you*" (italics added) are more accurate renderings. This may spoil some good sermons!

The common interpretation of the last clause of verse 8 emphasizes the close communion with God that is required if we are to receive His personal guidance for ourselves. Although this is not the *primary* meaning of this passage, nothing is lost, for the same truth is taught elsewhere. In Psalm 123:2 the servant is depicted as watching for direction from master or mistress: "As the eyes of slaves look to the hand of their master, as the eyes of a maid look to the hand of her mistress, so our eyes look to the Lord our God." Along with His promise of counsel—a very inclusive promise—the Lord says He will keep His eye on us, thus assuring us of His vigilant care.

The metaphor of bit and bridle combines the idea of guidance with restraint. You cannot counsel a horse or a mule! When people fail to respond to the gentler methods of the Lord, He must at times take stronger measures to save them from themselves. So He sends trials, troubles, and sometimes suffering. The purpose of bit and bridle is not to keep the horse from coming near us, but rather to bring it to us. This is the beneficent purpose of our Father when He resorts to the bit-and-bridle method. Trials are not meant to distance us from Him, but to draw us nearer.

I believe God has an individual will for my life and for every life, but its realization depends on a true surrender of *my* will and *your* will to Him for the fulfillment of His plan as and where He sees best. He may, however, leave considerable freedom of choice within His moral will, and He may choose to overrule our acknowledged mistakes to fit in with His will, as illustrated in the parable of the potter.

> Whate'er my God ordains is right,
> He never will deceive me,
> He leads me by the proper path,
> I know He will not leave me.
> I take content
> What He hath sent.

Summary

God has a plan for every life. Our circumstances are not accidental but are planned by Him. He is not aiming to produce facsimiles, but to develop each personality, so He treats us, not as robots, but as sons. Sometimes His dealings will seem mysterious at the time, but He has promised future explanation. Our wisdom and vision are finite, but His are infinite. Because of our limitations there will always be areas we don't understand. For this reason, we need a Guide through the maze of life. "It is not in man to direct his steps" is the dictum of Scripture. We need a Guide because the disposition of events is not in our hands. And the upsurge of demonic activity in our day makes His guidance even more necessary.

God has given many promises of personal guidance. If we wish to know what kind of Guide He is, we need only look at Christ, who has revealed the Father as a loving, compassionate, gracious, and forgiving God, not as an ascetic ogre whose delight is to say No! If we make a wrong decision, we are not doomed to a second-best life. He delights in giving another chance.

God's will is what He plans and purposes, and that will is our highest good. Paul describes it as "good, pleasing and perfect." Not everyone believes God has an individual will and plan for each life, but that is what the Bible seems to teach. Such a plan would not be like an architect's blueprint or a travel agent's detailed itinerary. God is not dealing in figures and places and times but with people whom He has endowed with free will, and He acts accordingly.

2. The Nature of God's Guidance

Key Topics:
- Principles of Guidance
- The Pillar of Cloud
- Putting Out a Fleece
- Negative Light on Guidance
- The Claim of Duty
- Conditions of Guidance

A yieldedness to the will of God is not demonstrated by some one particular issue: it is rather having taken the will of God as the rule of one's life. To be in the will of God is simply being willing to do His will without reference to any particular thing He may choose. It is electing His will to be final, even before we know what He may wish us to do.

It is therefore not a question of being willing to do some one thing; it is a question of being willing to do *anything,* when, where and how it may seem best in His heart of love. It is taking the normal and natural position of child-like trust which has already consented to the wish of the Father even before anything of the outworking of His wish is revealed.[12]

—*Lewis Sperry Chafer*

Principles of Guidance

It is an interesting fact that the impersonal word *guidance,* which is so often in our thoughts and on our lips, does not occur in the Bible. But there is a great deal said about God as a personal Guide. Rather than having impersonal guidance, we are promised the personal companionship of an experienced Guide to lead us through the maze of life. For a traveler passing through unfamiliar territory, a highly qualified guide is much to be preferred to a road map!

God's method of guidance in the past varied with the degree of development of the people He was leading. For Israel, a horde of slaves who had had no experience of living a free life, He provided a set of rules and regulations. But later, Jesus did not propound a set of laws for His people to follow. He gave them great moral and spiritual principles that they would have to apply themselves to the circumstances of life. He did not treat them as young pupils under a tutor, but as adult sons.

One of these unchanging and foundational principles is that *our Guide will never depart from the precepts of the Word of God.* In its pages we will find infallible guidance on all matters of spiritual, moral, and ethical importance. Where Scripture speaks clearly, no further guidance need be sought. For example in Ephesians 4:25 we are commanded, "Each of you must put off falsehood and speak truthfully. . . ." So everything that smacks of deceit and falsehood is out. Our path is clear.

Here are some other principles of guidance:

1. *In the whole of the Bible we are given commands and promises, prohibitions and warnings appropriate to any situation in which we find ourselves.* Hence the necessity of reading and studying the whole will of God as found in the whole Word of God.

As a young man I worked alongside a lawyer who made a practice of reading one of the thirty-one chapters of the book of Proverbs every day of the month to keep his business ethics straight and also to profit by the wisdom of Solomon. Those in other professions too might find this practice profitable.

The Old Testament is as important and valuable in gaining an understanding of God's will as the New. We will be more likely to find light on matters requiring decision in the course of daily Scripture reading than in a random dipping into it. We would not treat any other book of importance in a random way.

2. *It is in the place of prayer that God will impart His guidance to us.* The practice of our Lord is a sufficient example. Let us look at one instance: In choosing the twelve apostles, Jesus had to make one of the most important decisions of His whole career. He was to select the group of men to whom, after training, He would entrust His whole world enterprise that was to continue for millennia. On them in coming days would rest the failure or success of the whole venture. How important, then, that He choose the right men. He had many followers. How could He know with assurance if He had chosen the right ones?

> One of those days Jesus went out to a mountain-side to pray, and *spent the night praying to God.* When morning came, he called his disciples to him and chose twelve of them, whom he also designated apostles.
> *Luke 6:12–13* (italics added)

It was in prayer that He sought and obtained His Father's direction. All His prayers were answered because He asked only for things according to the Father's will and purpose (John 11:42).

It was also in the place of prayer that Samuel Logan Brengle discovered God's will for his life. He later became one of the most God-used men of the Salvation Army. As a roving commissioner he took revival wherever he went around the world.

Brengle was brought up in a godly Methodist home, but he had no ambition to be a preacher. He was ambitious, but his ambition lay in another direction. In the course of time he entered the university. "His purpose in entering was not to save souls, but to expand Brengle. The medium he had chosen for that expansion was oratory." It was a day of great orators in America, and the fever had gripped him.

He gained the first prize in oratory and became the university orator, representing his alma mater on many occasions. When it came to choosing a vocation, although he thought it would be wonderful to be a preacher, he wanted to achieve fame, so he elected to study law instead and looked forward to a political career.

Up to this point the idea of preaching—"the Call"—had followed him, but in 1882, "the Call stepped out of obscurity, blocked his path, demanded a decision." He had to make an important speech on behalf of his university at a university convention where vital issues were at stake. He was deeply burdened and could find no rest for his spirit. While he knelt in his room, lonely and depressed, the thought of preaching was suddenly presented to his mind. A tremendous inner battle ensued, but when at last he cried, "O Lord, if Thou wilt help me to win this case, I will preach!" the whole room seemed instantly to flame with light. The next day he delivered his speech, and to his intense surprise, his victory was sweeping.

When he told his closest friend, he said, "Sam, you'll be a fool to go into the ministry." But the die was cast. God had kept His part of the contract; Brengle too would keep his.

In the course of time, after further theological studies, he was presented with a call to a beautiful and influential church in Indiana. But he was convinced his call was to evangelistic work. Ultimately he gave up the idea of a pastorate, joined the Salvation Army (then a much despised organization), and became their first roving commissioner. He roamed the world, and everywhere he went, revival followed. He had not mistaken the guiding Light.

On God's method of preparing a man for His service, Brengle's biographer wrote,

> When He wants a Moses, He allows him to obtain his training and develop his legal sense in a worldly court. When He wants a Paul, He directs his ambitions along paths that give him a background of education, culture, pharisaism even. And when He wants a Brengle, He fills his soul with aspirations which, though at first they point to a selfish and carnal end, drive him onward toward the development of those powers which, transformed, will make of him what He desires.[13]

3. *It was while the church leaders at Antioch were praying and fasting that the Holy Spirit,* the Administrator of the missionary enterprise, *communicated His will to them.* "While they were worshiping the Lord and fasting, the Holy Spirit said, 'Set apart for me Barnabas and Saul for the work to which I have called them' " (Acts 13:2).
4. It is in submissive, expectant prayer that *our heavenly Guide imparts wisdom and insight* into the problems we face. It was for this that Paul prayed: "This is my prayer: that your love may abound more and more *in knowledge and depth of insight"* (Phil. 1:9, italics added). When we are facing major decisions, it is obvious wisdom to spend concentrated time in prayer.

5. *He guides us through the advice of wise and spiritually experienced friends* (even if we suspect they may give adverse advice). Solomon gives this counsel, "Listen to advice and accept instruction, and in the end you will be wise" (Prov. 19:20). Dialogue stimulates thought and broadens vision.

6. Sometimes *He guides by creating desires in our hearts* that accord with His sovereign purpose and moral will. ". . . for it is God who works in you to will and to act according to his good purpose" (Phil. 2:13). Because of our natural tendency to be biased in favor of our own view, we should carefully scrutinize our desires. Of course they may be of God.

7. *He guides us by exercising an inward constraint or restraint,* as he did with Paul and his companions on the way to Macedonia (Acts 16). He orders circumstances so that they either facilitate and confirm our plans or obstruct them.

8. *He guides through divinely imparted gifts and abilities,* both natural and spiritual. Our leading will generally accord with our gifts, but there are exceptions. It is here that spiritual gifts we are exercising with the Lord's blessing should be taken into account.

9. As treated more fully elsewhere, *He guides us through our minds.* We should be wary of any guidance that belittles or overestimates the use of the intellect. In response to the prayer of faith, the Lord imparts wisdom: "If any of you lacks wisdom, he should ask God, who gives generously to all" (James 1:5).

10. *He guides through the revelation of Christ* in His life and death. Jesus lived according to universal principles, so that the spirit of those principles can be lived out anywhere. His leading is not so obvious as to make our vital involvement in the process unnecessary. God leads, but He does not override the will of man. In guidance there will always be a need for our mental and spiritual exercise.

The Pillar of Cloud

In the process of leading His people Israel out of Egypt and into the Promised Land of Canaan, God used a method that suited that stage of the nation's development. It must be remembered that the Israelites had just emerged from four centuries of slavery. They had had no experience of any other type of life and were totally unsophisticated, so God employed the kindergarten pictorial method of instruction. One element of that was guidance through the desert by means of a pillar of cloud by day, which took on the appearance of fire by night.

> On the day the tabernacle, the Tent of the Testimony, was set up, the cloud covered it. From evening till morning the cloud above the tabernacle looked like fire. That is how it continued to be. . . . Whenever the cloud lifted from above the Tent, the Israelites set out; wherever the cloud settled, the Israelites encamped.
>
> *Numbers 9:15–17*

In the daytime it afforded welcome shade from the fiery sun, like a great umbrella. During the night it provided illumination. It went before them to show the way and followed behind them as a rear guard to protect them. But its irregular movements were not always to the people's liking.

> God's leading often crossed their inclinations,
> The pillar went too fast, or went too slow,
> It stayed too long to suit their restless temper,
> Or when they wished to stay, it bade them go.

The pillar of cloud guided them in all their long, thirty-eight-year trek, right to the borders of the Promised Land. But once they entered Canaan, the external manifestations of God's presence and guidance were withdrawn. The manna ceased, the cloud melted away, and the fire no longer glowed. God was leading the nation into a more mature relationship with Himself.

In his first letter to the Corinthians, Paul twice stressed the fact that the experiences of Israel on this trek had spiritual relevance for Christians in his day.

> Now these things occurred as examples to keep us
> from setting our hearts on evil things as they did.
> . . . These things happened to them as examples
> and were written down as warnings for us, on
> whom the fulfillment of the ages has come.
> *1 Corinthians 10:6, 11*

In the early stages of the Christian life, believers may experience more tangible evidences of God's presence and activity. As we grow in spiritual maturity, these may diminish, as God leads us more by enlightening our spiritual judgment. Jesus spoke of the blessedness of "those who have not seen and yet have believed" (John 20:29).

Israel's guidance came by means of the supernatural pillar of cloud and fire; ours comes by the reality of which the pillar was only a picture, a symbol. The distinctive feature of the pillar of cloud was that *God was in it,* controlling its every movement. Although they had no idea what lay ahead of them, the Israelites followed the stops and starts of the cloud obediently. They had to trust the skill and integrity of the God who controlled the cloud, and as long as they were obedient, their journey prospered. In this way God purposed that they should learn the lesson of complete dependence on Him for every step of the way. They had no option but to live a day at a time.

We have no supernatural cloud to guide us, nor do we need one, for we have a supernatural though invisible Guide who knows the way and goes before. "The steps of a man are from the Lord, and he establishes him in whose way he delights," said David (Ps. 37:23 RSV). And Jesus promised, "I am the light of the world. Whoever follows me will never walk in darkness" (John 8:12).

So long as the Israelites followed the cloud, they walked in the will of God. They had to be constantly on the alert—a useful lesson for us. If we set our minds on a certain course, it is easy for us, like British admiral Lord Nelson, to put the telescope to our blind eye, so that we cannot see the warning signal that our Guide flashes.

> God holds the key of all unknown,
>   And I am glad;
> If other hands should hold the key,
> Or if he trusted it to me,
>   I might be sad.
>   —*J. Parker*

We may well wonder how Moses and his aides managed to synchronize the movements of such a vast encampment. The answer is, their movements were regulated by the blasts of silver trumpets. "The Lord said to Moses: 'Make two trumpets of hammered silver, and use them for calling the community together and for having the camps set out' " (Num. 10:1–2).

It was the responsibility of the sons of Aaron to monitor the movements of the cloud and to order the people forward by blasts on the silver trumpets. If they failed to obey the summons, they forfeited the protection of the Lord. Not to move when the trumpet sounded would be tantamount to rebellion against the Lord. What does this have to say to us?

There is a lesson here for those in leadership. We are set as watchmen to relay the will of God to our people and to detect and foil the approach of the enemy.

Putting Out a Fleece

A remarkable incident in the life of Gideon has given rise to a contemporary practice for seeking guidance. It has come to be known as "putting out a fleece." Because of its prevalence, a careful study of its validity is warranted.

Repeated invasions by the Midianites and Amalekites had reduced the Israelites to desperate straits. So serious was their plight that they had resorted to living in caves and mountain strongholds. In response to their cry for help, God raised up an unlikely champion, Gideon, to deliver them. He commanded him to save Israel out of the hand of the oppressors.

> "But Lord," Gideon asked, "how can I save Israel? My clan is the weakest in Manasseh, and I am the least in my family."
> The Lord answered, "I will be with you, and you will strike down all the Midianites together."
> *Judges 6:15–16*

An amazed Gideon obediently gathered an army of 32,000 to fight the enemies who had assembled in the valley, "thick as locusts. Their camels could no more be counted than the sand on the seashore" (7:12).

It takes no vivid imagination to conceive the sense of total inadequacy that swept over the inexperienced Gideon when faced with such overwhelming odds. One can empathize with his desire for more tangible assurance than the bare word of an angel of the Lord. Gideon's state of mind can be gauged by his response to the Lord's assurance of His favor and promised presence. His reply contained two ifs.

> *"If* you will save Israel by my hand *as you have
> promised*—look, I will place a wool fleece on the
> threshing floor. *If* there is dew only on the fleece
> and all the ground is dry, *then* I will know that you
> will save Israel by my hand, *as you said."* And
> that is what happened.
>   *Judges 6:36–38* (italics added)

One would have thought that this remarkable sign of divine intervention would have been enough to dispel his fears and quicken his confidence in God. But no. God's gracious response did not satisfy him; he needed another sign. So, apologetically, he asked God to reverse the course of nature for a second time!

> "Do not be angry with me. Let me make just one
> more request. Allow me one more test with the
> fleece. This time make the fleece dry and the
> ground covered with dew." That night God did so.
>   *Judges 6:39–40*

But even this miracle failed to stimulate his faith or allay his fears. So, in grace, God arranged yet another way of bolstering his timorous servant's faith. He told him to go down to the Midianite camp and listen to what they were saying, and then he would be encouraged to attack the enemy.

Imagine Gideon's astonishment when he overheard a Midianite soldier tell his companion of a dream he had had in the night and of his interpretation of it: "This can be nothing other than the sword of Gideon son of Joash, the Israelite. God has given the Midianites and the whole camp into his hands" (Judg. 7:14).

The threefold compassionate response of the Lord to His timid servant casts a reassuring revelation of the character of our God. But it also reveals the unpromising material out of which He fashioned "a mighty man of valor."

Such are the facts. But is God holding up Gideon as a model for emulation? Are we justified in taking this incident as our model when seeking guidance? There is a divergence of opinion on the wisdom or legitimacy of this practice.

On the positive side, it does reveal God's graciousness in a very moving way. Also, whatever his motivation, Gideon did exhibit an admirable desire to be sure of God's will. The Lord's positive response showed His recognition of that desire. But it did not necessarily indicate His approval.

On the negative side, there is a strong case against the contemporary practice of "putting out a fleece" or asking God to give or confirm guidance by some providential or supernatural sign. It is true that many have put out their fleeces (the author among them) and have received a positive response from a gracious God. Doubtless many more will do the same. But when all is taken into account, wasn't Gideon's experience God's compassionate response to an unfounded doubt, rather than a response to Gideon's faith? "And without faith it is impossible to please God" (Heb. 11:6).

In considering the validity of adopting this method of seeking guidance, the following factors should be taken into account:

1. There is no New Testament parallel to Gideon's fleece test. A secular parallel in our day would be tossing a coin a second time because it did not turn up the way we wanted the first time. It was a special sign to Gideon, but not necessarily to us.

2. In reality, Gideon was not seeking guidance in the strict sense. *He already knew what God's will was.* The command was clear and unequivocal. He admitted this by his statements, "as you have promised" and "as you said" (6:36, 37). When God gives a command, no further guidance is necessary.

3. God's gracious response did not dispel Gideon's distrust of God's plighted word. God had to grant a second sign to

bolster his faltering faith (7:13–14). (He may have thought there could have been a natural explanation of the phenomenon.) *"Fleece-setting" does not impart final assurance and certainty.* As someone said, "If the Word of God is not enough for you, fleeces will also leave you in doubt." Our part is to trust and obey.

4. Some consider a spectacular response to setting a fleece an evidence of superior spirituality. But is it not rather a gracious concession to feeble faith? Gideon was in effect saying to God, "I have your word of promise, but I'm not sure I can trust it without some tangible evidence." Of course he would not put it in those words, but that is what it amounted to. In asking for a reversal of the course of nature, he was demanding guidance on his own terms. Jesus said to Satan, "Do not put the Lord your God to the test" (Matt. 4:7).

So from a study of the incident, there appears to be little support for adopting this practice, although God in His love and patience toward us slow-learners may have compassion on our tremulous faith. Jesus pointed out the better way: "Blessed are those *who have not seen* and yet have believed" (John 20:29, italics added).

Negative Light on Guidance

An Old Testament incident gives negative instruction on our theme. It concerns King Balak of Moab and the ambivalent prophet Balaam.

During its desert journey, Israel was enabled by God to inflict a crushing defeat on the cruel and idolatrous Amorites (Numbers 21:25–26). When King Balak and his people heard of this victory, they were in a state of panic.

> Moab was terrified because there were so many
> people. Indeed, Moab was filled with dread
> because of the Israelites.

> The Moabites said to the elders of Midian,
> "This horde is going to lick up everything around
> us, as an ox licks up the grass of the field."
> *Numbers 22:3–4*

Balak had heard of the fame of the prophet Balaam, so in superstitious fear he summoned him to put a curse on the Israelites and thus secure their defeat. Of course there would be an adequate reward.

If he were a true prophet of Jehovah, Balaam should have dismissed the proposition out of hand and sent the delegation packing, back to the king. God's command was so clear and unequivocal that there were no grounds for postponing giving them a final answer. "You must not put a curse on those people, because they are blessed" (22:12) were God's words.

But Balaam toyed with temptation, for he "loved the wages of wickedness" (2 Peter 2:15). So he left the door open for a further approach from Balak. Parleying with temptation is always fraught with danger. The serpent should be killed, not stroked.

> The perils that we well might shun
> We saunter forth to meet;
> The path into the road of sin
> We tread with careless feet.
> *—J. Bright*

So categorical a command from God should have closed the matter for Balaam, but he was held captive by the lure of money and was loath to send the delegation back to the king firmly and conclusively.

Balak, refusing to take no for an answer, dispatched an even more prestigious delegation and promised an even more generous reward. Balaam tried to persuade the Lord to change His mind and allow him to go to Balak. When God saw that he had determined to secure the reward, whatever the cost, He went to him in the night and said, "Since these men have come to summon you, go with them, but do only what I tell you" (22:20). It was when he was on his way with the princes to King Balak that the mysterious incident of the talking donkey was enacted.

Had God changed His mind? Not for a moment. Since Balaam refused to take no for an answer, God said in effect, "If I cannot keep you from disobeying me, go, and reap the consequences." There is a limit to the divine patience with one who tries to get the best of both worlds.

Although the Lord was angry with him for his intransigence, in mercy He tried to prevent him from taking the irrevocable step. The encounter with the angel and the unusual behavior of the donkey were a further endeavor by God to save him from his folly. But even that dramatic event did not deter him.

Reluctantly, Balaam finally confessed, "I have sinned" (22:34), but his subsequent behavior gave those words a hollow ring. He had trifled with his conscience until its voice became muted and ceased to transmit faithful warnings. The end result of Balaam's persistent disobedience was that, when he could not bend God to his will, he stooped to advocate the seduction of God's people. A number of contemporary lessons about guidance may be drawn from this story:

1. Balaam is a warning beacon to any who formulate their own plans and then try to get God to sign on the dotted line.

2. We must avoid the mistake of equating God's permission with His express will. Balaam made that mistake with tragic consequences.

3. Motivation is an important element in guidance. Balaam was deflected from the clear path of duty by the lure of money.

4. When God has clearly indicated His will—and a great deal is clearly spelled out in the Scriptures—yet we toy with the temptation to pray again in the hope of inducing God to give a different answer, we are on dangerous ground.

5. It is infantile behavior to plague God with a repeated request in the hope that He will change His mind and approve our plan.

6. We should thank God for His restraining providence if He places roadblocks in our way when we are acting contrary to His will.

7. Balaam desired to "die the death of the righteous" (Num. 23:10), but his unrighteous lifestyle and his love of money resulted in his being killed by the Israelites whom he had betrayed and seduced.

The Claim of Duty

In considering avenues along which guidance may come to us, we should not overlook the claims of simple duty. Thomas Carlyle gave a sage piece of advice in this context: "Do the duty that lies nearest to you which you know to be your duty. Your second duty will already have become clearer."

Our Lord's earthly life was marked by a strong sense of duty. The word *duty* appears but seldom in the New Testament, but the idea is very prevalent. Even when He was only twelve years old, Jesus was conscious of a divine imperative in His life. When at last His parents found Him after a three-day search of the streets of Jerusalem (Luke 2:41–50), He was in the temple "sitting among the teachers, listening to them and asking them questions."

"Son, why have you treated us like this?" His mother asked Him.

To her half-chiding question, Jesus asked in surprise, "Why were you searching for me? Didn't you know *I had to be in my Father's house?*" (italics added).

Early in His ministry, the people of Capernaum brought to Him those suffering from all kinds of diseases, "and laying his hands on each one, he healed them" (Luke 4:40). Seeing the possibility of their city becoming a lucrative and famous health spa if only they could retain Jesus' services, "they tried to keep him from leaving them. But he said, *'I must preach the good news* of the kingdom of God *to the other towns also, because that is why I was sent"* (Luke 4:42–43, italics added). He refused to be localized, but bowed to the claims of duty. His whole life was a model of splendid devotion to duty.

The same strong sense of duty characterized Paul even before his conversion and was still more prominent afterward. When making his defense before King Agrippa, he said, *"I too was convinced that I ought to do all that was possible* to oppose the name of Jesus of Nazareth" (Acts 26:9, italics added).

Obedience to the claims of duty will do much to clarify the confusion of thought that often clouds the guidance process. As Martin Luther said, "We don't need to look beyond the obvious responsibilities of our vocation for guidance. We should assume that its details are a daily sermon." *It is our duty to do our duty. That simple fact takes care of a large area of life for which no further guidance need be sought.*

When adherence to duty becomes a permanent principle of life, much will already have been done to simplify the decision-making process. "He did his duty as a horse eats oats," was said facetiously of the Duke of Wellington. It will be found that the genuine call of duty and the voice of God do not conflict.

Once we have decided on or taken up our vocation or other area of commitment under the guidance of God, we will find that He usually gives guidance in the normal course of that commitment. If He does move outside that area, we can expect Him to make it unmistakably clear. So when seeking to know the will of God in any situation, one important preliminary question is, "What is my clear duty?"

Dr. R. A. Torrey relates that a man came to him and said that God was leading him to marry a certain woman. He described her as a devoted Christian. They had been greatly drawn to one another and felt that God was leading them to be married.

"But you already have a wife," said the evangelist.

"Yes," was the reply, "but we have never lived happily, and we have not lived together for years."

"But that does not alter the case," the evangelist replied. *"God in His Word has told us distinctly the duty of the husband to the wife,* and how wrong it is for a husband to divorce his wife and marry another, except in the case of adultery."

"Yes," responded the man, "but the Holy Spirit is leading us to one another."

"Whatever spirit is leading you to marry one another, it is certainly not the Holy Spirit, but the spirit of the evil one. The Holy Spirit never leads anyone to disobey the Word of God."

It is a striking fact that where God has given supernatural guidance, it has seldom been asked for. "In most cases God intervenes unexpectedly and gives a person guidance even when no request has been made for it. In other words, God goes 'out of His way' to make sure the person has adequate knowledge of His will in order to do it."[14]

Consider three outstanding leaders in Israel's history—Moses (Ex. 3), Saul (1 Sam. 9–10), and David (1 Sam. 16:1–13). In not one instance had they any prior indication that they were to be selected for leadership. *The guidance came unsought while they were simply doing their duty* in the mundane activities incidental to their ordinary vocations. This pattern is perpetuated today.

Conditions of Guidance

The Scriptures prescribe no infallible and inflexible set of rules to be followed in order to qualify for being admitted into the mystery of the will of God. But there is an attitude of heart and mind that is a prerequisite to guidance. "He guides the humble in what is right and teaches them his way" (Ps. 25:9). The "humble" who thus qualify are those who are distrustful of themselves, who desire to be taught, and who are prepared to follow the divine leading whatever the cost. The basic attitude is submissiveness. There is no divine guidance for those not willing to do God's will.

To the Jews who were amazed at the knowledge of the carpenter from Galilee, Jesus spelled out the condition for knowing the will of God. *"If anyone chooses to do God's will,* he will find out whether my teaching comes from God, or whether I speak on my own" (John 7:17, italics added).

The clear lesson is that knowledge of the divine will is dependent on the attitude of the human will. The person who has made the basic choice of doing God's will instead of his own will be in a position to prove the validity of Christ's words and promises. Obedience to God's will so far as it is known will enable one to enjoy the Spirit's illumination of the Word.

At a conference in Ben Lippen, South Carolina, a young woman who was heading for the mission field was invited to give her testimony. In the course of doing so, she held up a sheet of paper, blank except for her signature at the bottom. "Here is the plan for my life," she said. "I have signed it at the bottom, and I am leaving it to God to fill in the details."

It was a naive concept, and she would still have to work her way through the guidance process. Just in heading for work among the unevangelized of the world, she was doing God's will. She had graphically demonstrated her confidence that He would guide her as she made future decisions.

A surrendered will implies that we are as willing to have our plans vetoed as to have them confirmed by our heavenly Guide. This attitude is not always reached overnight. Sometimes it will come only after many prayers and much soul-travail. But divine obligations must always take precedence over personal preferences. Where there is a conflict of interests, the verdict must always go in the Lord's favor. We will seek guidance in vain if we have already made up our minds.

The story is told of an old Scotsman who went to his lawyer to ask advice on a certain matter. After hearing the problem, the lawyer gave his opinion. The old Scot said, "Thank you," and began to walk away.

"Wait a minute," said the lawyer. "You haven't paid my fee!"

"Your fee?" queried the Scot.

"Yes, for my advice."

"But I'm not taking it!" rejoined the client.

Many seek the Lord's guidance, but in their hearts they have no intention of following it if it does not please them.

It has been my privilege to preach several times in an American church that has a remarkable history. It is a large church and has spawned six large and thriving daughter churches. It was commenced by the man who pastored it for about thirty years. The story of his early years illustrates some of the points we have been discussing.

Marvin was in his third year at Bible college and was working part time in an athletic goods store to pay expenses. One day a stranger entered and asked, "Are you Marvin?"

"I admitted my identity," Marvin related some time later, "wondering who he was and what he wanted.

" 'They told me I would find you here.'

" 'Well, you found me.'

"He looked me over and said, 'Will you go down to Switzerland County, Indiana, next Sunday and preach for a little country church, morning and evening services?'

"With no hesitation, my answer was a forthright, 'No, I won't.'

" 'If you don't accept this request, the people will have no preacher next Sunday.'

"I replied, 'They won't have one if I accept.'

"He didn't smile at my humor. 'Listen,' he said, 'they have asked me to obtain help. I have asked everyone I know. Someone told me you might go for just one Sunday. I know you are a third-year student. You must have at least two sermons you could preach. What do you say? Will you go?'

" 'Okay, I'll do it, just for this one Sunday,' I heard myself saying. When he left I felt a little sick. I didn't want to preach, I wanted to be a Christian football coach. Was there a power at work in my life, a Hand that opened doors and shut doors, and provided situations?"

He entered the little church an hour before the time of the service, and an immense, overpowering feeling of destiny pulled him to his knees before one of the chairs.

"My prayer was informal: 'Lord, here I am, about to preach to forty or fifty farm people who raise tobacco for a money crop. I am lonesome and homesick. I want to go to college and learn to coach boys, but I don't want to preach. I need your help to get me through this day. O my God and Father . . .' Tears came. I just wept and stayed there.

"It was as though a Hand was laid on my shoulder. 'O God,' I prayed, 'I think I see a little clearer. You want me to preach. You want me to give up my plan and accept yours. You have been closing doors and opening doors, gently leading me to this very place. Well, if you have gone to this much trouble, I promise you that I am willing to look for further signs of your leading.'

"Fifty-seven people came. They listened and made no comment. Most returned that evening. When it was over a senior elder said, 'Would you mind waiting outside? We want to have a little meeting.' By and by he opened the door and said, 'Come back in.' The people were all grinning at me. I thought the meeting was to tell me I would never make a preacher. I knew that already and just grinned in return.

" 'We want you to come back next week,' the elder said.

" 'I have already told you all I know; what would I say next Sunday?'

"He replied, 'You'll come up with something. We think you will be a fine preacher, and we want you to preach for our little church.'

"I started to lift my hands as though in defense, and back away, but then I remembered my prayer of a few hours earlier: 'O God, I am willing to follow your plan.' "[15]

Summary

God's method of guiding His people varies with their degree of development. He led Israel through its desert trek by the kindergarten pictorial method—a pillar of cloud and fire and a set of rules. Now He leads His people by the principles of His Word and by their own intelligence, enlightened by the Holy Spirit. His guidance is received in the place of prayer, as our Jesus demonstrated in His own life. The Lord guides through the advice of friends, the creation of holy desires, through the exercise of inward restraint, the imparting of wisdom, and our native abilities and spiritual gifts. He also guides through the revelation of Christ and the spirit of the universal principles to which He himself submitted.

The pillar of cloud was a sign to Israel, though not necessarily to us. Our guidance comes through the reality of which the pillar was a symbol. And although God graciously reversed the course of nature twice at Gideon's request, that was a concession to his weak faith, not a model for us to follow. The story of Balaam is a warning beacon to anyone who tries to wheedle God into doing what he or she wants.

The simple claims of duty also afford clear guidance. It is our duty to do our duty. Both Jesus and Paul did so meticulously. Where duty is clear, no further guidance is needed. Yet guidance is conditioned. One main requirement is willingness to do God's will. Knowledge of God's will is dependent on the attitude of our will. God guides the humble in heart.

3. Contributory Elements in Guidance, One

Key Topics:
- The Impregnable Rock of Scripture
- The Ministry of the Counselor
- The Place of Prayer
- The Involvement of the Intellect
- The Function of Conscience

> God does not want to guide us magically, He wants us to know His mind. He wants us to grasp His very heart. We need to be soaked in the content of Scripture, so imbued with biblical outlooks and principles, so sensitive to the Spirit's prompting, that we will know instinctively the upright step to take in any circumstances small or great. Through the study of Scriptures, we may become acquainted with the ways and thoughts of God.[16]
>
> —*John White*

The Impregnable Rock of Scripture

If God Himself is the chief factor and actor in guidance—and He is—then His holy Word comes second in order of importance. It must be given precedence over every other element in the guidance process.

The Impregnable Rock of Holy Scripture is the title of an old book, and a very insightful title it is. For centuries the criticisms and attacks of succeeding generations of its foes have swirled around God's Word, but it stands firm and immutable. Our feelings ebb and flow, but the Bible remains invulnerable, reliable, trustworthy. When God has spoken, there is no more to be said.

Through the devout reading and study of the Scriptures we learn authoritatively the thoughts and ways of God, and His will for daily living. In the canonical Scriptures, His basic revelation of Himself and His will is complete, and we are warned against accepting any other professed revelation as authentic and authoritative.

Hear the solemn words of warning in the final chapter of the whole book:

> I warn everyone who hears the words of the prophecy of this book: If anyone adds anything to them, God will add to him the plagues described in this book. And if anyone takes words away from this book of prophecy, God will take away from him his share in the tree of life and in the holy city, which are described in this book.
> *Revelation 22:18–19*

The teachings of Scripture form our basic guide, and *in them most of God's will for daily living is already revealed.* The Bible is a compendium of principles, precepts, prohibitions, and promises and is therefore our most important point of reference. The instructions that are recorded are not given as a set of rules to be slavishly followed, but as principles that are applicable to all the circumstances of life.

Paul makes this claim for the Scriptures: "All Scripture is God-breathed and is useful for teaching, rebuking, correcting and training in righteousness, so that the man of God may be thoroughly equipped for every good work" (2 Tim. 3:16).

But while all Scripture is useful and profitable for all, every part is not equally applicable to all. It is important to keep this in mind in our interpretation of passages that bear on our subject. Some passages have reference to specific conditions that are applicable only to that particular situation. The prophecy of the fall of Jerusalem foretold in Luke 21:20–24 is a case in point.

Interpret Scripture in Context

In our interpretation we must take account of the context, the problem discussed, the historical and cultural setting. By taking texts out of their context, one can prove almost anything from the Bible. But as we study it reverently and expectantly, the Holy Spirit, who inspired it, will illuminate and authenticate its message to us.

He will show us the relevance of certain passages or principles to our daily walk and to the matter about which we are seeking guidance. For example, in the Sermon on the Mount, Jesus demonstrated to the Pharisees and scribes that the Ten Commandments are surprisingly wide in their application (compare Ex. 20:3–17 with Matt. 5:17–48).

Then again, certain promises are made to specific people or groups, times or places. It is wrong to pluck historical statements of fact from their context and try to fit them to our own circumstances. That often leads to absurdity. However, Paul does assure us that the Old Testament promises are our spiritual inheritance.

> There is neither Jew nor Greek, slave nor free, male nor female, for you are all one in Christ Jesus. If you belong to Christ, then you *are Abraham's seed, and heirs according to the promise.*
>
> *Galatians 3:28–29* (italics added)

Mere intellectual knowledge of the will of God insofar as He has revealed it in Scripture is not sufficient. Scripture must be internalized in some way, such as Jeremiah described when he said to the Lord, "When your words came, I ate them; they were my joy and my heart's delight" (15:16). God delegates to us the responsibility of using our sanctified intelligence to work out the best application of the biblical principles to our own situation. In this we have the Holy Spirit as our Helper.

The Bible does not claim to legislate in detail for every matter of conduct that may arise. Instead, clear principles of conduct are enunciated. When correctly applied, these will be found to cover most contingencies—but we must work at searching them out. If God had not made clear guidance available to us, how could He hold us responsible if we failed to do His will?

Dr. Raymond Brown, who was principal of Spurgeon's College in London, England, tells of the way in which the call of God came to him as he was reading his Bible: "It was natural, I suppose, that during the first few months of my new sphere as an airman I should think deeply about what the Lord really wanted me to do with my life. That was, after all, an interim occupation. I would not always be doing it.

"At that time God spoke clearly to me about full-time Christian work and clearly convinced me that I was to expound His Word.

"The call came suddenly, on a summer Saturday evening when, as a young serviceman, I sat in Liverpool Central Hall waiting for a meeting to begin. As I sat quietly reading my Bible, the vivid story of Isaiah's call suddenly became my own, and I knew from that moment that I too must preach.

"I have not the slightest idea what went on in the meeting that followed. I sat or stood as the others did, but my heart and mind were somewhere else. I was totally incapable of thinking of anything else than this undeserved privilege. With a sense of stunned wonder, I emerged from that meeting knowing that I must give my life to the proclamation of the biblical message."

God can speak to us clearly and satisfyingly while we are quietly reading His Word.

However, there is a wrong use of Scripture. It is not to be used as a sort of horoscope or crystal ball. In guiding us, God does not bypass the intellect He has endowed us with. The Bible is a reasonable, well-attested book that has satisfied the most brilliant intellects of those who have read it objectively. While God is willing to help us in areas beyond our mental capacity, *He does not do the thinking for us!* The Holy Spirit will enlighten our minds when we ask Him to and sincerely desire to do God's will. But we must beware of the pitfall of *reading into* Scripture a meaning that cannot reasonably be *read out* of it.

Charles H. Spurgeon, in his graphic way, said:

> What is the mariner without his compass? And what is the Christian without the Bible? This is the unerring chart, the map in which every shoal is described, and all the channels from the quicksands of destruction to the haven of salvation mapped and marked by the One who knows all the way.

The Ministry of the Counselor

In His office as Christ's Vice-regent on earth, the Holy Spirit is necessarily deeply involved in the guidance process. Because He is both inspirer and illuminator of the Word of God, we can count on His help in understanding the guidelines laid down that lead to insight into the will of God.

> In the same way, the Spirit helps us in our
> weakness. We do not know what we ought to pray
> for, but the Spirit himself intercedes for us with
> groans that words cannot express. And he who
> searches our hearts knows the mind of the Spirit,
> because the Spirit intercedes for the saints *in
> accordance with God's will.*"
>
> *Romans 8:26–27* (italics added)

As Jesus promised the gift of "the Counselor," He assured His disciples, "When he, the Spirit of truth, comes, he will guide you into all truth" (John 16:13). It is therefore not without significance that our understanding the will of God is linked with the ministry of the Spirit, specifically with our "being filled with the Spirit."

> Be very careful, then, how you live—not as
> unwise but as wise, making the most of every
> opportunity, because the days are evil. Therefore
> do not be foolish, but *understand what the Lord's
> will is.* Do not get drunk on wine, which leads to
> debauchery. Instead, *be filled with the Spirit.*
>
> *Ephesians 5:15–18* (italics added)

Three things are emphasized in these verses:
1. Knowing the will of God is not so much a matter of the emotions as of the understanding, the mind.
2. Understanding what God's will is makes one wise. "Live as wise . . . understanding what the Lord's will is."
3. Being filled with the Spirit enables one to know the will of God.

A person who is drunk on wine is sometimes said to be "under the influence." The Spirit-filled Christian is under the influence and control of the Spirit, for that is the meaning of the word "filled."

We laypeople talk of alcohol as being a *stimulant,* but in his book *Life in the Spirit in Marriage, Home and Work,* Dr. Martin Lloyd-Jones, a distinguished physician as well as a preacher, says it clearly is not a stimulant. In pharmacology, alcohol is classified as "a *depressant,* because it depresses the highest centres of all in the brain. These centres control everything that gives one self-control, judgment, balance, the power to assess everything that makes man behave at his very best and highest."

On the contrary, unrestrained, the use of alcohol makes a man lose control and behave like an animal—a tragic fact of which we are reminded every day.

Indwelling and Infilling

In contrast, a life lived under the control of the Holy Spirit produces the winsome "fruit of the Spirit" (Gal. 5:22–23). This ministry of the Spirit releases our inhibitions and progressively changes us into the likeness of Christ (2 Cor. 3:18).

The tense of the verb "be filled" in Ephesians 5:18 indicates a continuous action, so we are commanded to keep on being filled with the Spirit—so yielded to Him that He can control, empower, and guide us.

It should be noted that we are nowhere commanded to ask for the *indwelling* of the Spirit. That began upon conversion. He is our permanent, indwelling Guest. "You, however, are controlled not by the sinful nature but by the Spirit, *if the Spirit of God lives in you.* And if anyone does not have the Spirit of Christ, he does not belong to Christ" (Rom. 8:9, italics added).

Another two Scriptures that are in current use in connection with guidance are Galatians 5:18 and Romans 8:14. In each verse the clause "led by the Spirit" appears. What is its meaning? When the expression is interpreted in its context, it has no implicit reference to guidance. The Romans passage is concerned with resisting the impulses of the sinful nature and the Galatians passage with divine sonship.

Then what is meant by being led by the Spirit in the guidance process?

1. As we "walk in the Spirit," He will progressively *develop in us "the mind of Christ"* and enable us to adopt His lifestyle. It is an accepted fact that persons who live together for a long time, grow increasingly like each other. As we have seen, Christ dwells in us by His Spirit, and to the degree we allow Him to control our lives, He will form the mind of Christ in us. To do His will will be our delight.

2. He will *give us insight* into the guidelines that are laid down in Scripture for us.

3. He will *throw light on the biblical models* we ought to emulate and, equally, give warning about those we should abhor.

4. He will *make the will of God a joy* and a delight, instead of a burden to be accepted reluctantly.

5. He will *aid us in selecting a goal* toward which we should direct our energy—a goal that will bring glory to God and blessing to others. The achieving of this goal will be a source of great joy and profit to us.

6. He will sometimes *exercise His negative authority* and veto projected plans that He sees will, in the long run, not contribute to His glory or to our highest interests. He did this with Barnabas and Saul when they attempted to preach in Mysia and Bithynia (Acts 16:6–7). This was not out of caprice; the strategy of the Holy Spirit was that the good news should reach Europe first. His guidance was not all negative, however, because He did lead them to Macedonia.

7. While the Holy Spirit is versatile in the methods He adopts in working with men and women, those methods generally

conform to the laws and structures of the human mind. Occasionally we are the subject of an instinctive movement, but usually man's powers of perception and judgment form the basis of human action.

"Guidance, while similar to the teaching work of the Holy Spirit," writes John F. Walvoord, "has a different character. While the teaching ministry of the Holy Spirit in this age is directed to making clear the meaning of the Word of God, guidance is making the application of the truths thus known. Guidance is always deductive, that is, the application of general principles to the particular problem at hand. . . . In the many details of each life, only the Spirit of God can provide necessary guidance."[17]

8. Stephen Winward comments that the Spirit will *urge us gently* when we are moving in the direction of the will of God: "It will eventually be found that the Spirit gives a *gentle urge* in a certain direction. Perhaps a door clearly opens (or equally clearly closes); or there is a deepening inner conviction of a line of action to be taken. This will prove sufficient to indicate the next step. As that step is taken, the way will gradually, step by step, open out. There will be an increasing sense of confidence which leads to the apparently puzzling, yet true, statement so often made that 'Guidance is easier to see when we look back than when we look forward.' "

The Place of Prayer

> I urge, then, *first of all,* that requests, prayers, intercession and thanksgiving be made. . . .
> *1 Timothy 2:1* (italics added)

Prayer and guidance are to be regarded as Siamese twins. They cannot exist apart. In view of the scriptural injunction, ". . . *in everything,* by prayer and petition, with thanksgiving, present your requests to God" (Phil. 4:6, italics added), time must be set apart for seeking God's face.

The question naturally arises, "Since God is sovereign and knows our needs before we ask Him (Matt. 6:8), why the need of prayer? Why doesn't He just give us what we need?" The answer C. S. Lewis gave to one who posed this question was this: "God could have chosen to do His work in any fashion He wanted, but He chose to do it (in part) in response to prayer."[18] Prayer indicates dependence on God.

It would be presumptuous to expect God to reveal His will to us if we expressed no desire to know and do it. If we are in deep earnest about finding His will for our lives, we will be willing to make sacrifices to spend time in His presence so as to gain His perspective on things. It is in sincere and sensitive prayer that God imparts wisdom and insight or guides us to appropriate passages of Scripture. In the place of prayer the Holy Spirit is able to get His message through to us.

> Jesus, Savior, pilot me
> Over life's tempestuous sea;
> Unknown waves before me roll,
> Hiding rock and treacherous shoal;
> Chart and compass come from Thee,
> Jesus, Savior, pilot me!
> —*Edward Hopper*

We should place whatever matter about which we are seeking guidance trustfully and completely in the Lord's hands, not hesitating to spell it out in detail and to lay before Him our feelings and concerns. In no subject are we more conscious of our lack of wisdom than in prayer. But our Father has made provision for this very lack.

> If any of you lacks wisdom, *he should ask God,*
> who gives generously to all without finding fault,
> and it will be given to him. But when he asks, *he*
> *must believe and not doubt,* because he who
> doubts is like a wave of the sea, blown and tossed
> by the wind. That man should not think he will
> receive anything from the Lord.
>
> *James 1:5–7* (italics added)

The immediate context here suggests that it is wisdom to know what to do in the face of trial that James has in mind, but his language is so general and inclusive that it can be taken as including wisdom of every kind. With this assurance beneath our feet, we can approach the making of decisions with confidence, "For the foolishness of God is wiser than man's wisdom" (1 Cor. 1:25).

If we are genuine in our purpose to know God's will and do it, our prayer may result in a redirection of desire and a strengthening of purpose. Was this not the result of our Lord's prayers in Gethsemane?

In His first petition He referred to His (human) will and His Father's (divine) will: "My Father, if it is possible, may this cup be taken from me. Yet not as I will, but as you will" (Matt. 26:39).

In His second prayer, however, the dichotomy between the two wills has disappeared: "My Father, if it is not possible for this cup to be taken away unless I drink it, may your will be done" (Matthew 26:42).

Why the difference in the petitions? What had happened? In the crucible of His agonized praying, He had received the revelation of His Father's will for Him. Submissively He yielded, and merged His human will with that of His Father. His submission was not reluctant but willing, as His exclamation showed: "Shall I not drink the cup the Father has given me?" (John 18:11).

What was the answer of God's love
Of old, when in the Olive Grove
In anguish—sweat, His own Son lay,
And prayed, "O take this cup away?"
Did God take from Him then the cup?
No, child. The Son must drink it up.

—Ibsen Brand

What an example for us to follow! Sometimes we are confronted with two alternatives, one of which runs counter to our desires, yet seems to be the Lord's will for us. What should we do? If we pray, "Lord, at the moment I am not willing to do this, but I am willing to be made willing," the Lord will perform the miracle, redirect our will, and with our consent merge it with His own.

When facing an important decision with far-reaching implications, it is also a great strength to enlist the prayer support of a few trusted friends who know the power of prayer.

So we may say that prayer directed by the Holy Spirit is the principal means of obtaining guidance. Through prayer we can check any guidance we may appear to have received. Where there is no true praying in the Spirit, there will be little experience of the guidance of the Holy Spirit.

The Involvement of the Intellect

On special occasions in Old Testament times, God appeared to His people to give them guidance. Apparently He spoke in an audible voice directly to the prophets and others. It was this method of communication that He adopted with young Samuel:

Then the Lord called Samuel.
Samuel answered, "Here I am." And he ran to

Eli and said, "Here I am; you called me."

But Eli said, "I did not call; go back and lie down. . . ."

The Lord came and stood there, calling as at the other times, "Samuel! Samuel!"

Then Samuel said, "Speak, for your servant is listening."

1 Samuel 3:4–5, 10

In New Testament days, that mode of communication was infrequent. It was largely superseded by the exercise of the believer's judgment, instructed in the principles of the Word of God and under the illumination of the Holy Spirit.

In referring to his own experience of discerning the will of God, the wise John Wesley said, "God generally guides me by presenting reasons to my mind for acting in a certain way." Notice that he did not say "by presenting feelings to my heart." Emotion has its place but should never be allowed to be a paramount factor in guidance.

As we pursue His guidance, *God never asks for the abeyance of our intellect.* We are not to become robots. There are some anti-intellectual and ultraspiritual persons who consider that the use of reason and the full exercise of the intellect in such matters are unspiritual. But God does not intend His promised guidance to be a mechanical substitute for our mental effort. He has endowed us with brains, and He expects us to use them—but always in subjection to the principles of His Word and under the control of the Holy Spirit. He can guide only a submissive mind and will.

Thoughts proceeding from a sanctified and biblically-orientated mind are likely to be the will of God for us. But even sanctification does not render our minds infallible. Our conclusions should be checked by the Scriptures, the counsel of competent advisers and the confirmation of the Holy Spirit.

The Exercise of Common Sense

If we are "walking in the Spirit" and in communion with Christ, our commonsense decisions in the ordinary duties of life will most likely prove to be the will of God, unless there is a distinct, inward correction from the Holy Spirit, such as Paul and Barnabas experienced en route to Troas. If we saturate our minds in the Scriptures, our decisions will be the product of a Spirit-illumined and Spirit-guided mind.

There may be rare occasions when God asks of us something that seems to be contrary to common sense. There are a number of biblical incidents that would fall into that category. One striking example is the Lord's command to Noah to build a huge, seaworthy vessel in an area far removed from the sea—a project that would take one hundred and twenty years! No wonder Noah was included with the other heroes of faith in God's Roll of Honor in Hebrews 11! He implicitly obeyed the divine command and thus saved the human race from destruction.

Yet we should beware of any teaching that advocates a passive and blank mind while seeking guidance. That smacks more of demonism and the use of mediums than divine leading.

Paul sought to bring his every thought into subjection to Christ. "We take captive every thought to make it obedient to Christ" (2 Cor. 10:5). In guiding us, the Holy Spirit does not ignore the minds God gave us, but speaks to our intelligence and understanding.

John R. Mott was an intellectual and one of the great student leaders in the early years of this century. He was a prime mover in the Student Volunteer Movement, which through its motto—"The Evangelization of the World in This Generation"—motivated thirty thousand students to become missionaries.

His biographer records a letter he wrote to his father when he was facing the critical decision of how he was going to invest his life. I quote it at length, for it portrays the interplay of the Word of God, the Spirit of God, and an intellect brought under the control of the Holy Spirit.

"In these days a man cannot afford to make any mistakes. Every decision a man makes shapes his entire after life. As I look back over the few years I have been making decisions, I can see how true it has been in my case.

"I have tried to give this question fair examination as well as much prayer that my decision may accord with God's will. That is all I want to be assured of—that I am acting in accordance with His unerring plans.

"There are two things I desire to convince you of in my life. First, that I do not jump at a decision, but consider it from all sides, getting advice from every reliable source, and then reaching from the conflicting opinions my own decision.

"Second, that I am not led by others, even by a large majority, unless they happen to be in harmony with my standards of decision:

(a) The Holy Spirit, who guides by cooperation with

(b) the Scriptures

(c) Reason, not feeling

(d) Conscience

(e) Providential events.

"I never regretted a decision I made by these guiding standards. If you have them on your side, what matters it if the whole world is against you for God is on your side? And if God be for you, who can be against you?"[19]

Paul counseled Timothy to exercise his mental powers and so gain insight into the truth he had been imparting. "Reflect on what I am saying, for the Lord will give you insight into all this" (2 Tim. 2:7). The Holy Spirit works through our diligent study of the Word of God.

In the account recorded in Acts 8:26–40, Philip discerned the voice of God and obeyed promptly. When he arrived at a junction in the road he met an Ethiopian eunuch, an important official in charge of all the treasury of Candace, queen of the Ethiopians, engaged in reading Isaiah 53. The seemingly foolish interruption of Philip's previous activities began to make sense. True, he had left a local revival, but he had been sent to be instrumental in giving the gospel to the African continent. Sometimes God's leading is beyond reason but it is never contrary to reason.

If on a rare occasion God asks us to do something which does not seem to accord with common sense, we can expect some special indication from Him. However, we should remember that God's will will not always make sense to the non-Christian, or even to a Christian who is not "walking in the Spirit." We should check such guidance by prayer, by Scripture, by wise counsel, and by the constraint of the Holy Spirit. Guidance that seems to go against common sense should be followed only if God gives clear and definite leading.

> When Paul prayed for his converts and so set the pattern for us, he prayed that they might "be filled with the knowledge of his will in all spiritual wisdom and understanding" (Col. 1:9 RSV). He did not pray that they might "feel led" to enter the path in which God wished them to walk. As the human response to God in man's struggle for highest obedience, greatest spiritual power and most mature growth, Paul urged the

exercise of the sanest type of intelligent apprecia-
tion of God's desires.[20]

The Function of Conscience

What part does conscience, that persistent monitor of the
soul, play in guidance? It fills a very important role. In view
of the influence it has on our emotional well-being and its
frequent mention in Scripture, surprisingly little attention is
paid to it in preaching and writing.

A study of the relevant Scripture passages indicates that
conscience is a special activity of intellect and emotion that
enables one not only to perceive moral distinctions, but also
to discriminate between good and evil. It is the faculty within
us that decides about the moral quality of our thoughts,
words, and acts. So its activity impinges upon our perception
of the moral will of God.

It is the activity of conscience that makes our sin
culpable. The word signifies "knowledge held in conjunction
with another," and of course the other is God. Conscience
makes us co-witnesses with God against ourselves.

We must not, however, regard conscience as an executive
faculty, for it has no power to make us do right or to keep us
from doing wrong. *Its sole responsibility is to deliver its
verdict according to its own standards and produce the
appropriate emotion.* A thermometer would be a good
parallel. It registers and indicates the temperature but has no
power to create or modify it.

Conscience is not infallible, for it can react only to the
standards it knows. It is a safe guide only when it has been
instructed by the Word of God. Hence the importance of daily
study of the Bible.

Its unreliability when not instructed by the moral and
spiritual standards of Scripture was seen in the men who

committed the horrors of the Inquisition. The consciences of the men who perpetrated those horrible tortures actually commended them for what they did. They reacted according to the accepted standards. The delicate mechanism of conscience was thrown off balance at the Fall, and now it requires constant adjustment to God's standards. The reactions of our consciences will vary according to the accuracy of the adjustment.

A Commending Conscience

Paul lists three progressive, positive conditions of conscience.

A clear conscience

A clear conscience is one that is acutely conscious of the approach of evil. Paul had to strive to keep his conscience clear; that was, and is, not automatic. "So I strive always to keep my conscience clear before God and man" (Acts 24:16). He maintained its purity by obeying the dictates of Scripture and the promptings of the Holy Spirit.

A good conscience

". . . holding on to faith and a good conscience" (1 Tim. 1:19). A good conscience commends the right and condemns the wrong. It is the possession of one who obeys the dictates of the clear conscience.

A mature conscience

"How much more, then, will the blood of Christ, who through the eternal Spirit offered himself unblemished to God, cleanse our consciences from acts that lead to death, so that we may serve the living God!" (Heb. 9:14). Now, with a good, clear, cleansed conscience, the believer can give himself or herself without any sense of condemnation to the service of God.

A Condemning Conscience

Paul also had a list of progressive, negative conditions of conscience.

A weak conscience

This type tends to be morbid and overscrupulous and is easily upset by trifles. A weak conscience is perpetually self-accusatory. "Some people are still so accustomed to idols that when they eat such food they think of it as having been sacrificed to an idol, and *since their conscience is weak,* it is defiled" (1 Cor. 8:7, italics added).

The corrective action would be to face the issues involved, make a decision according to one's best judgment, and then resolutely refuse to open the matter again.

A defiled conscience

If we willfully persist in engaging in some activity against which conscience has protested, we thereby defile it and hinder its faithful functioning, just as dust in the mechanism of a watch will cause it to register the wrong time. This is especially the case where moral purity is involved.

A guilty conscience

". . . having our hearts sprinkled to cleanse us from a guilty conscience" (Heb. 10:22). A guilty conscience results from the habitual disregard of the warnings of conscience. It results in its possessor having values so warped that he calls evil good and good, evil.

A seared conscience

"Such teachings come through hypocritical liars, whose consciences have been seared as with a hot iron" (1 Tim. 4:2).

> Men say: I think this course is right because my conscience does not reprove me. Therefore it is right for me. Nonsense. Jesus told His disciples that some day men would kill them. "A time is coming when anyone who kills you will think he is offering a service to God" (John 16:2). He pointed out that there is such a thing as moral colourblindness (Matt. 6:23).[21]
>
> —*Robert E. Speer*

Summary

Scripture is one of the most important factors in guidance. It is God's final word, and His guidance will never contradict its teaching. Where God has spoken clearly and unequivocally in His Word, no further guidance is needed. He has left it to us to apply its principles in our own situation. Most of God's will is revealed for us in Scripture, but its statements and promises must be interpreted in their context.

The Holy Spirit, whom Jesus called "the Counselor," fulfills this office for us. He inspired the Scriptures and, as we rely on Him, throws light on the relevance of certain passages to our situations. In Ephesians 5, understanding God's will is linked to being filled with the Spirit. He exercises both a constraining ministry and a restraining influence when we are not in line with His will. Sometimes He vetoes our plans, because He has something better. He gives special help in the area of prayer. Prayer and guidance are Siamese twins. At times as we pray He will redirect our will as He did Jesus' in Gethsemane. Prayer directed by the Spirit is the main channel of guidance.

God never asks us to let our minds go blank, for that opens the door to alien forces. Our intellects have been given to us to use, but in subjection to the Spirit. God may on occasion ask someone to do something that seems *beyond* reason, but He will never ask us to act *irrationally.* Conscience fills an important role, but it is not infallible, and its verdicts should be checked by the standards of Scripture.

4. Contributory Elements in Guidance, Two

Key Topics:
- The Value of Counsel
- What Part Do Circumstances Play?
- Where Do Our Desires Fit In?
- Evaluation of Gifts and Abilities
- The Influence of Temperament

> If we are honest, we shall never be certain that our motives are absolutely pure. We know our own hearts too well. In such a decision we must pray for a true objectivity and ask God to give us such an overriding desire for His honour and glory that we are able to judge aright. But it is no good indulging in endless introspection. We must make allowances for our own selfishness and get on.
>
> By all means we must pray about it, and ask to be given a willingness which does not come naturally to us, and a fresh love for Him which makes selfish considerations small. But then we must turn to the objective task of seeking out the divine wisdom of the matter, determined that, by God's grace, we will obey whatever is right.[22]
>
> —*Oliver R. Barclay*

The Value of Counsel

> Plans fail for lack of counsel, but with many advisers they succeed. (Proverbs 15:22)

> Listen to advice and accept instruction, and in the
> end you will be wise. (Proverbs 19:20)

So counseled the wise man! Many who have neglected taking his advice have lived to rue the day. Experience proves that wise and godly counsel is one of the most valuable channels of guidance. There are many decisions that can safely be made unilaterally, but the more complex they are the greater the advisability of taking counsel.

In my early years I had little hesitation about making decisions unilaterally, but I soon learned the wisdom of Solomon's proverb, "Make plans by seeking advice; if you wage war, obtain guidance" (Prov. 20:18). I have learned the value of dialogue and consultation, for they stimulate thought, broaden vision, and give deeper insight into the issues at stake.

But advice is only as good as the one who gives it, so one should give careful thought to the question of whom to consult. Here are some recommended guidelines:

• Choose some mature person or persons in whom you have confidence, who will be able to give objective and biblical judgment.

• Avoid approaching someone whom you are sure will give advice along the lines you want to hear. In other words, someone who is so involved as to be likely to lack objectivity. King Ahab is a warning beacon. When Ahab was seeking guidance, he consulted only the prophets whom he was sure would approve his course. All four hundred of them agreed with him! There is danger in selecting counselors we are sure will not run counter to our desires.

• Beware of incompetent or inexperienced advisers.

• In a major decision it would be wise to seek advice from more than one person.

• Don't avoid seeking advice from someone who might give adverse counsel. It is good to hear the negative as well as the positive side of the case.

• Consult Christian parents—and non-Christian parents, too, if they have a strong Christian ethic.

• Don't accept the advice tendered as final in reaching your decision. Check it against other factors.

• Don't allow your counselor to make the decision for you. It is for you to decide, for it is you who will, for good or ill, have to live with its results.

A young woman approached Dr. E. Stanley Jones asking his advice concerning a choice she had to make between two men who were courting her, and whom he knew.

"Do you think I should marry this man, or that one," she asked.

"I think you should marry neither," replied Dr. Jones. "Neither is worthy of you."

"There, that settles it!" was her rejoinder. "Last night I told God I would take your answer for His answer."

"Wait a minute," said Dr. Jones, "I am not God! This is my opinion. The choice is yours."

"It is right to ask advice of others," wrote Dr. R. E. Speer, "to consider their views, to measure the consequences of different courses of action. We should leave no means of inquiry or investigation unused, *in order to be sure what is right.*

"But when we have found it, we are to do it, just because it is right, not because of what others say about it, or because of what the consequences may be. Friends may counsel against our folly. They did that in the case of Christ."[23]

> If it is right, there is no other way!
> This is the voice of God, the call of truth;
> Happy the one who hears it to obey,
> And follows upward, onward from his youth.

There can be such a thing as too much counsel. Going from one counselor to another may just be an indication of unwillingness to take responsibility for the possible results of the decision. This attitude is infantile. The time comes when procrastination must no longer be tolerated and the nettle of decision must be grasped.

What Part Do Circumstances Play?

Is it right to assume that favorable circumstances constitute the will of God for us? Undoubtedly they play an important part in the process of guidance, but they should not be taken as final without confirmation by other indicators.

Jesus told His disciples that the Creator God, who controls the rolling orbs of space, does not fail to note the fall of the humble sparrow. He is a sovereign God who never relinquishes control of circumstances, not even the actions of wicked men. Potentates and politicians may pride themselves that they are making history and may create great libraries to perpetuate their achievements. But Paul cuts them down to size when he writes, "He [God] fixed the epochs of their history and the limits of their territory" (Acts 17:26 NEB). As Sovereign Lord of the Universe, He controls the circumstances and orders them as He will. And His will is good. "Moreover we know that to those who love God . . . everything that happens fits into a pattern for good" (Rom. 8:28 Phillips).

When God declared, "O house of Israel, can I not do with you as this potter does? . . . Like clay in the hand of the potter, so are you in my hand, O house of Israel" (Jer. 18:6), He was expressing His absolute control of events and circumstances. The poet Robert Browning expressed this conviction:

> He placed thee 'mid this dance
> Of plastic circumstance,

> Machinery just meant
> To give thy soul its bent,
>   Try thee and turn thee forth
>   Sufficiently impressed.

No circumstance comes to pass by chance, although its significance may not be apparent at the time. Later it may be seen as a vital factor in the unfolding of a life plan. This was so with the author.

As a young man, I applied for admission to the Bible Institute of Los Angeles and asked them to send the appropriate forms. In due course I received a reply from the registrar saying that he was sending the material under separate cover, but it never arrived. At the time I wrote that letter, I did not know that a Bible college had been founded recently in New Zealand. In the waiting period, I met some of its students, who encouraged me to enroll there. In the providence of God, I later became principal of the Bible College of New Zealand for a number of years. God had overruled an office glitch in Los Angeles to direct me into His plan for my life.

The lesson is that, when we trustfully commit our way to the Lord as we are urged to do (Ps. 37:5), we can confidently expect Him to order the circumstances and to guide us to opportunities that are in line with His plan.

The Time Factor

He controls the time factor. In reading the Scriptures one cannot but be struck with the meticulous accuracy of the timing in certain important incidents. Take, for example, the "chance" meeting of Philip the Evangelist with the Ethiopian eunuch, who "chanced" to be reading the greatest gospel passage in the Old Testament when Philip's path "chanced" to cross that of Candace's Minister of Finance. What great issues hung on Philip's prompt obedience to the divine command. Five minutes' delay in obeying the call of God, and their paths never would have crossed, and the continent of Africa would have had to wait longer for the Good News.

When the circumstances are in keeping with the tenor of Scripture, and coincide with the informed judgment of the believer and the inner conviction of the Holy Spirit, then they serve as a confirmation of the choice made. In decisions of far-reaching importance, especially, circumstances should play only a minor part. Coincidence never negates God's command. Circumstances alone should never be taken uncritically as the will of God.

While I was writing this chapter I received a letter from a friend enclosing a quotation that he said had been a great blessing to him and to many with whom he had shared it:

> The Lord may not have planned that this should overtake me, but He has most certainly permitted it.
>
> Therefore though it were an attack of an enemy, by the time it reaches me, it has the Lord's permission and therefore all is well.
>
> He will make it work together with all life's experiences for good.

Where Do Our Desires Fit In?

One of the perplexing problems faced by one who sincerely desires to know and do the will of God is to determine the part that his or her personal desires should play in the decision-making process. How should our choices be influenced by our subjective feelings? The problem is further compounded for some by the unjustified fear that if we desire a thing strongly it most probably is not God's will. If this is one's view, this distorted impression of the nature of God should be dealt with first. God is not a "Celestial Killjoy." It is the consistent teaching of Scripture—and the experience of saints throughout the ages—that God is more willing to guide us than we are to be led.

There is a current saying, "Love God and do what you like." Is that a scriptural concept? *Ideally,* if all of us loved God with all our heart and soul and mind, that may be legitimate, for we would all then desire to do only what He wanted. But we do not live in an ideal world, and who among us is ideal in his or her actions and reactions? We do not automatically do what God desires. Sometimes God desires what we do not like! We need a more objective basis for important decisions.

The psalmist correctly revealed the will of God when he wrote, "Delight yourself in the Lord, and *he will give you the desires of your heart"* (Ps. 37:4, italics added). The implication is that as we delight in daily close fellowship with the Lord, He for His part will grant our desires. "He fulfills the desires of those who fear [reverentially trust] him" (Ps. 145:19). So if our ambition is—as it should be—to please the Lord, our desires may well be an indication of His will.

Jesus claimed, as recorded in John 10:4, that His sheep follow Him because they know His voice. God is actively at work in our hearts and minds to create in us desires that are compatible with His eternal purpose. "It is God himself whose power creates within you both the desire and the power to execute his gracious will" (Phil. 2:13 Weymouth). It is the function of the Holy Spirit to give birth to desires that lead to holy activity. If our desires are good and holy, they may very well be seeds of the Lord's planting.

Yet, if we are deeply involved emotionally in the alternatives we are considering, it is not at all difficult to project our subconscious desires as the voice of God. How are we to distinguish between the two? Here are some suggested procedures that might clarify the issue:

1. Discard the myth that if you desire something, God most likely does not.

2. Believe God's promise that He will give light to those who are willing and who strive to do His will, no matter what it is (John 7:17).

3. Ensure that the course you desire to pursue is legitimate biblically and is according to the tenor of Scripture.

4. Consider whether or not your desire runs counter to your primary and obvious duty.

5. Determine whether or not competent counselors support your plan.

6. In making your decision, ask in faith for the wisdom promised in James 1:5.

If your desire passes these tests, then you have good grounds for believing it to be the will of God for you.

Evaluation of Gifts and Abilities

How far should our gifts, abilities, and training influence us in our decision-making? Observation would indicate that God *generally* guides along the lines of the natural gifts and abilities with which He has endowed us. To these the Holy Spirit adds spiritual gifts that prepare us for the work of the kingdom.

A spiritual gift is not a natural ability but a special operation of the Holy Spirit in the life of the Christian, whereby He employs his or her personality for a spiritual purpose. It is more than a natural gift and frequently transcends one's natural abilities. In considering matters of guidance, we should take into account our actual or potential abilities and skills, but they alone should not determine the issue.

No believer is without some spiritual gift. "Now *to each one* the manifestation of the Spirit is given for the common good. . . . All these are the work of one and the same Spirit, and he gives them *to each one,* just as he determines" (1 Cor. 12:7, 11, italics added).

So each believer has a special gift from God and may in fact have more than one. But often these gifts lie latent and are never exercised. Some hold the view that these gifts are temporary and are later to be withdrawn. Scripture nowhere makes this point; it is at best an inference. We must also be aware that spiritual gifts can be abused. Their primary purpose is to build up the church. Therefore, the test of any such gift is: Is it resulting in the upbuilding, enrichment, and unity of the church?

Some venture to engage in major activities for which they have displayed no aptitude, with the erroneous assumption that this is walking by faith. In fact it is more likely to be presumption. If God were leading a person to do such a thing, He could be expected to make His will known by giving more than ordinary guidance and very deep inner conviction.

In His sovereignty, God does at times take someone who is spiritually equipped, but who seems ill-equipped by natural gifts, to use him or her in areas that would otherwise be closed to that person. One striking illustration of this is the ministry of a man I know, who is spiritually mature and who has for many years been the national leader of Youth for Christ in New Zealand. From the natural viewpoint, he would be disqualified for such a position because he has a severe stammer. In ordinary conversation it is always present, but when he steps on the platform or the TV stage, the stammer disappears, only to reappear when he steps off.

I once asked him why he thought the Lord had entrusted him with this disability. "Oh, I know," he answered. "He wanted me to be more than ordinarily dependent on Him." Each time he speaks in public is a fresh act of faith, and God has responded greatly to his trust. But such cases are exceptional, and it is unusual for God to use someone significantly in an area in which he or she has shown no competence.

Then does this disqualify an inexperienced person from undertaking Christian work for which he or she has had no previous experience? Certainly not, or no one would begin! But we should first be willing to prove our competence in minor areas before venturing to undertake a major assignment.

The Influence of Temperament

The decision-making process will take its character, in part, from the temperament of the person involved. Temperament has been defined as a person's nature as it controls the way he or she behaves, feels, and thinks. It is the soul's essential response to its surroundings.

Just as no two persons have identical fingerprints, so no two people have identical temperaments. The traditional view is that there are four types of temperament—sanguine, choleric, melancholic, and phlegmatic. However, there is no such thing as a pure type; we are all hybrids! But one type usually predominates in a personality.

People of different types will approach and evaluate a situation in different ways, just as two or more persons seeing the same auto accident will give different descriptions. The four main types of temperament may allow individuals to come to the same conclusion, but each will process the information in a different way. A helpful treatment of this subject is Tim LaHaye's *Finding the Will of God*.[24]

A brief description of each of the four types may be useful to our discussion. The following characterizations are, of course, oversimplified and widely generalized, and remember, there are no pure types.

Those of *sanguine* temperament tend to live in the present and are easily moved emotionally. Because of this, they are more prone to make emotion-based decisions and are likely to be less objective than others in their judgments. People of this type should be aware of the danger of being over-subjective and inconstant.

People of *choleric* temperament are sensitive and deep, and they tend to be goal-oriented. They are dependable, and their decisions will be influenced greatly by whether or not those choices fit their goals. They may be uncompromising and irresolute.

Melancholic people are very strong-willed and courageous individuals who tend to be introverted and perfectionistic. They are of a practical disposition and would decide in favor of the tough challenge.

Those of *phlegmatic* temperament are easygoing, calm, and practical. They tend to be slow and indecisive, but they make good counselors because they take time to listen to all sides of a problem.

We inherit our temperaments and cannot change them. But both Scripture and experience testify that the adverse elements of temperament can be ameliorated, or even eliminated, under the tutelage of the Holy Spirit. He does so in the life of one surrendered to His control by producing the fruit of the Spirit described in Galatians 5:22–23.

Summary

Solomon counseled us, "Listen to advice and accept instruction, and in the end you will be wise" (Prov. 19:20). When seeking guidance, the advice of a competent counselor is invaluable. Counselors should be biblically astute and should be able to give an objective assessment, pointing out the weaknesses as well as the strengths of our inclinations.

But it is not for the counselor to make the decision. Providential circumstances are also factors in guidance, but they too should not be the deciding element. They should be checked against other guidelines. At times, He sovereignly uses someone we would disqualify, but this is very much the exception. God keeps the time factor in His own hands.

It is sometimes difficult to differentiate our desires from God's will. Our desires may or may not be of His making. He has promised that if we delight in Him, He will give us the desires of our heart. That is the condition. He usually, though not always, leads us along the lines of our natural abilities. Our abilities do affect our guidance. Spiritual gifts are for the upbuilding of the church rather than for personal enrichment.

We all have inherited a temperament, which we cannot change. But its adverse aspects can be ameliorated by the Holy Spirit imparting His fruit. Temperament influences the manner in which we approach the decision-making process. There are four basic temperaments, but most of us incorporate qualities of more than one type.

5. Dreams, Visions, and Impressions

Key Topics:
• Supernatural and Spectacular Guidance
• Impressions and Intuition

> God does not lead His children by any rules whatsoever. No two of his children will be led alike, and it is most probable that He will never lead any one of His children twice in exactly the same way. Therefore rules are apt to be misleading. True spirituality consists in a life which is free from law and which is lived, to the minutest detail of individuality, by the power of the Spirit.
>
> The divine leading is by the Spirit who *indwells* the Christian. It follows therefore that true leading in this dispensation will be more by an inner consciousness than by outward signs. After we have faithfully met the conditions of the spiritual life, we have "the mind of the Spirit." He is able both to convince us of what is wrong and to impart a clear conviction of what is right.[25]
>
> —*Lewis Sperry Chafer*

Supernatural and Spectacular Guidance

In religious literature, instances of spectacular or apparently supernatural guidance abound. Some are reliably authenticated, others are not so well attested. Many readers of this book may well have had some such experience themselves.

In the Scriptures it is recorded that at times God used dreams or visions to communicate with His servants, but these were far from being everyday occurrences. We should not accept such incidents as final evidence of divine leading without further confirmation. It is a wise working principle to regard supernatural or spectacular guidance as the exception, not the rule.

One factor to be borne in mind is that at the time the biblical events were recorded, the New Testament was not in existence. But now we have the whole Bible, which contains the whole will of God in understandable terms, and the Holy Spirit Himself to interpret it. So such methods of communication have become less essential. Nevertheless, God is sovereign in this area as in every other, and it is not for us to say what He will or will not do.

In Old Testament times God revealed His truth to His people in pictorial form, as with the tabernacle of the testimony. He also used dreams and visions to convey His message to selected people. But it should be noted that they were mainly given only to holy men and women in the service of God, and usually they were unsought. However, Luke does record several accounts of visions received in New Testament times, so they cannot be ruled out.

John Wesley gives a word of advice concerning our attitude toward such manifestations:

> Do not hastily ascribe things to God. Do not easily suppose dreams, voices, impressions, visions, or revelations to be from God. They may be from Him, they may be from the devil. Therefore do not believe every spirit but try the spirits whether they be of God.

He rightly draws our attention to the fact that we have a wily adversary who has access to our minds and hearts. Peter, addressing Ananias, asked, "How is it that Satan has so filled your heart that you have lied to the Holy Spirit?" (Acts 5:3).

This fact should emphasize the necessity of walking in close fellowship with our Guide, who knows and can forewarn us of Satan's tricks.

In our times when so many are turning to the Eastern mystical religions for guidance, special care should be exercised. Mystical visions should not be sought. God's method is not mystical, but He communicates with us through mind and spirit. It is perilously easy to engage in self-hypnotism.

Supernatural Guidance Is Not the Norm

Since we now have both the Word and the Spirit, there is a strong case for affirming that the type of guidance we are discussing in this chapter is not normally to be expected. There is no instruction in either Old or New Testament that we should seek this type of guidance. God advocates the way of faith.

In her book *A Slow and Certain Light,* Elisabeth Elliott has this to say about miraculous guidance:

> There is one thing we ought to notice about these miracles. When God guided by means of the pillar of cloud and fire, by the star of Bethlehem, by visitations of angels, by the word coming through dreams and visions and prophets and even through an insulted donkey, in most cases these were not signs that had been asked for. And when they were asked for, as in the case of Jehoshaphat and Ahab, they were not accepted.
>
> Supernatural phenomena were given at the discretion of the divine wisdom. It is not for us to ask that God will guide us in some miraculous way. If, in His wisdom, He knows that such means are what we need, He will surely give them.

Peter's Unwelcome Vision

The vision that came to Peter, recorded in Acts 10:9–23, is sometimes advanced by those who seek visions as a means of guidance. An objective study of the passage, however, reveals that its purpose was not so much to direct him where to go, as to overcome his bitter Jewish prejudice against the Gentiles.

God's heart was reaching out to the Gentiles as it had to the Jews, and He wanted to make them, too, beneficiaries of the Good News. Cornelius the centurion was the key to the situation, but the Jews despised the "Gentile dogs" and would not even enter their homes.

God wanted to use Peter as His messenger, but Peter was deeply infected with this Jewish prejudice. He was a prisoner of his own cultural background, so God employed this unusual method to shock him out of his unreasoning prejudice. It is noteworthy that the vision appeared three times.

It was not the vision that directed Peter to the house of Cornelius, but the voice of the Spirit. "The Spirit said to him, 'Simon, three men are looking for you. So get up and go downstairs. Do not hesitate to go with them, for I have sent them'" (Acts 10:19–20). Note that he had been in prayer shortly before the Spirit spoke to him.

Peter did not seek the vision. It was a sovereign act of God sent for a specific purpose—the removal of a prejudice that was keeping Peter from doing the will of God. It is possible that sometimes when we think we are standing for principle, in reality we are falling for prejudice.

Because Peter heeded the object lesson of the vision, he was privileged to use the keys to open the door into the kingdom of God to the Gentiles, even as he had done for the Jews on the Day of Pentecost. The Spirit of God fell on those who were in Cornelius's house, thus demonstrating that the wall of partition between Jew and Gentile had been broken down.

There are biblical incidents in which God revealed His will and gave guidance through dreams in both Old Testament and New Testament. But examination reveals that these dreams did not usually come to people in general but to special people in special situations. Dreams are the outcroppings of the subconscious mind and often reflect repressed desires or fears. God may—and sometimes does—use this method in our day.

One modern instance of guidance through a dream with happy consequences is recounted of Dr. Tom Lambie of the Sudan Interior Mission. When home on furlough after one term of service in Ethiopia, he was faced with the offer of a lucrative medical partnership with his uncle, who would soon pass the whole practice on to him. Surely he could serve the Lord as an influential medical man at home as well as he could if he were buried in Africa!

He wrestled with the matter until one night a dream—so vivid that it seemed more than a dream—helped him decide. In the dream, a foul, leprous hand such as he had often seen in Ethiopia rose out of the heart of Africa, and a voice repeated, "Take that hand." Finally he went forward, and, though nauseated even in his dream, took the hand in his. As soon as he grasped it, it became the lovely, pierced hand of the Lord Jesus![26] The result of the dream was that he returned to Africa to become one of the field directors of the SIM.

Ulla Fewster is a missionary with Overseas Missionary Fellowship in Thailand and is involved in literature work. One night, with a missionary friend, Maj-Lis, she attended a prayer meeting in Bangkok, where they met Jean and Marian Bolton, who were half-time missionaries, but who had to support themselves by being secretaries.

When shaking hands, Marian said, "But we have met before!"

"I didn't think so," Ulla explained later, "but for a time we both tried to think where we could have met—all without result. During the prayer meeting, however, Marian whispered to Jean, 'Do you remember that dream I told you about three weeks ago?' Yes, Jean remembered.

"Marian dreamed that she had entered a building where several little groups of students were sitting around tables with a teacher in each group. Two teachers stood out in the dream, so clearly that Marian could describe them to Jean. One of them was me!

"Jean and Marian did not say anything about the dream to me, but they invited us to dinner a few days later. I can still remember—no feel—the goose pimples on my arms as I entered that house. There was a still, small voice inside me, God's voice, saying to me 'Ulla! this is where you are to live, and you are to work with these girls.' I still knew nothing of Marian's dream, of course.

"I said nothing to them, but I did tell Maj-Lis on the way home.

" 'Let's go back and tell them,' she exclaimed.

" 'No, no, how could I? Just compare their home with ours . . . .' I was afraid they would think I wanted a nicer house to live in.

" 'Let's pray about it for a week,' Maj-Lis suggested. 'If at the end of the week you still feel their house is the place for you, then I will go with you and tell them.'

"A week later we went back to Jean and Marian's home, and with trembling fingers I pressed the doorbell. Jean was at home and received us with pleasure.

" 'Well, Jean,' I said, 'I might as well out with it first as last. When I was here that evening I felt as if God was telling me that this is where I am to live, and that I am to work with you.'

" 'That's all right,' said Jean, 'we knew this already. We just wanted *God* to be the one to tell you. 'Then she told us about Marian's dream. We were amazed, and full of awe and gratitude to God."[27]

God does sometimes employ unusual methods of making His will known, but that is a matter for His sovereignty, not my demand.

Dr. R. T. Kendall succeeded Dr. Martin Lloyd-Jones as minister of Westminster Chapel in London. He wanted spectacular guidance, but it was only when he surrendered to the unspectacular that he discerned the will of God.

He had had no call to preach, but in his university studies he took subjects that would prepare him for either law or the ministry of the Word. One day a Scotsman named John Sutherland Logan spoke at the morning chapel service. Dr. Kendall thought at the time that it was the greatest preaching he had ever heard.

To his delight, Dr. Logan was asked to stay on the campus and hold services in a local church. Dr. Kendall went to hear him every evening. He introduced himself and talked with him after each evening service. He took Dr. Logan to breakfast before he left the campus.

"I have often said that I waited for Michael the Archangel to come down from heaven to tell me I was called to preach," said Dr. Kendall, "but God sent a Scotsman instead! Dr. Logan virtually told me, 'You *are* called to preach. I'm telling you that you are. Now go to your pastor and ask him to give you a local preacher's licence. Don't wait another day.' He signed his name in my Bible and added, 'Whatever he says to you, do it.'

"God used Dr. Logan to show me that I was wrong to demand the spectacular. He had that canny Scottish instinct

that detected how deeply I longed to be God's minister. I do not know if he ever gave anyone else advice like he gave me. All I know is that Dr. Logan was right. And yet I was disappointed. There would be no vision. No angelic voice. No great presence. Only a Scotsman saying, 'You are called to preach.' *It was surrender to the unspectacular that gave me peace* that I should prepare at once for the ministry."[28]

Impressions and Intuition

Seeking guidance through our fluctuating, subjective feelings is a very precarious method of determining the will of God. "I feel led" is a shaky basis for an important decision, for our feelings are so vulnerable and vacillating. Yet in testimonies, that is constantly advanced as the reason for a decision.

Our emotions do fill an important role in the decision-making process, for we are sentient beings. Yet because emotions are vulnerable to many external influences, they are very unreliable and variable indicators. For this reason alone, it is unwise to regard our present feelings as primary and dependable guides. A change of circumstances tomorrow—fatigue, ill health, unemployment, bereavement—could set off a whole new set of emotions. Any of a host of factors could play havoc with our feelings. So it is the opposite of wisdom to base a decision solely on our subjective emotions, important though they are.

But when we base our decisions on the objective reality of the unchanging Word of God, we are on safe ground. All subjective guidance should be cross-checked by more objective standards. As we have seen, John Wesley recognized this necessity when he shared his experience: "God generally guides me by presenting reasons to my mind for acting in a certain way."

Some people place a good deal of reliance on their intuitions, their "hunches," as a basis for guidance. It must be admitted that there are some whose intuitions are remarkably accurate, but there are many more whose hunches led them far astray. Our intuitions will be no more accurate than the knowledge we have gleaned that informs them. In any case, our intuitions are not precise gauges even of our own real feelings. "When intuition speaks," says one writer, "my subconscious has processed the information more quickly than the conscious mind, and my intuition is telling me what my subconscious mind has concluded."

We learn God's will, mainly, not by impulses and impressions, but by the prayerful study of the principles of Scripture and by their intelligent application to the case at hand.

Although our impulses and impressions are not to be equated with the voice of God, they are not to be disregarded in decision-making either. But they must be scrutinized and tested. One helpful guideline to apply is this: "God will never lead us into any course that does not fit the character and teaching of Christ." We might also ask ourselves, "Is this impression or impulse for the glory of God?" or "Is it consistent with the spirit of love?"

T. C. Upham maintained that "impulses and impressions from the Holy Spirit are of a peaceful and gentle character. They never disturb or agitate the mind, but lay a wholesome restraint on it. Impressions and impulses not of the Holy Spirit are not of a peaceful and quiet character, but are hasty and violent."

Another writer on this subject said that he had found no example in either the Old or the New Testament where it is clear that anyone had discerned the will of God by inward guidance. He maintained that cases that seemed so were either instances of supernatural guidance or of rational decision.

That God cannot and does not give impressions as one element of guidance is not suggested. But the only impressions that should be recognized as proceeding from God are those that are scripturally appropriate and are not contrary to sound wisdom.

I would personally deny my own experience if I were to say that God never guides by impressions. Yet I must affirm that they have to be tested, as well. On one occasion I was conducting a series of meetings in the Philippines. There were two meetings still ahead, but suddenly I had an extraordinarily strong conviction that I should cancel these meetings and go to a town in Australia where my nephew, to whom I had stood in the place of a father, was manager of a regional hospital. I knew he was ill but had no other information. I was able to make other arrangements for the meetings before flying to Australia. When I arrived at my nephew's home, there was no one there. Soon my niece arrived, and when she saw me she threw herself into my arms. She was at her wits' end. Her husband was seriously ill in the hospital and had had to resign his position. They were living in a house owned by the hospital and would have to leave within six weeks to make room for his successor. My nephew had managed the family's money, and his wife did not know the state of their finances.

I was able to ascertain how things stood and what sort of housing they could afford. Within twenty-four hours we had secured a suitable property and made the necessary arrangements. The next morning a friend came over and handed us a check for six thousand dollars as an interest free loan to my nephew. Then I was able to fly to my next appointment.

Normally, I would have been very wary about acting on an impression like that, but Jesus said that His sheep hear and are able to distinguish His voice. I had recognized His voice. After all, I had been hearing it for fifty years!

Summary

In Old Testament days God sometimes spoke to the prophets and to others in an audible voice, as He did to Samuel. He also used dreams and visions to illumine His will, but these were not everyday occurrences. With the completion of the Bible, the descent of the Spirit, and the advance of civilization, these methods of communication gave way to more personal guidance. While not ruling it out entirely, we should regard supernatural and spectacular guidance as the exception. John Wesley said that God generally guided him by presenting reasons to his mind (not feelings to his heart). Our fickle emotions are a shaky basis for an important decision. Supernatural phenomena have been given at the divine discretion. Peter neither sought nor welcomed the vision of Acts 10, which was given to remove his Jewish prejudice rather than to provide guidance.

Emotion does play a part in guidance, but because our emotions are variable and are vulnerable to outside influences and circumstances, it is unwise to base a decision *solely* on feelings and impressions. These should be tested by more objective standards. We cannot equate intuition with the voice of God. Our impressions may in fact be from God, but they should always be scrutinized and tested. "Is this for the glory of God?" is a primary test question. Acceptable impressions are scripturally appropriate. Impressions from the Holy Spirit do not disturb or agitate the mind.

6. Guidance in Mission

Key Topics:
- Paul's Missionary Vision
- The Missionary Call
- At Home or Abroad?
- Is a Special Call Necessary?
- Suggested Procedure for Missionary Candidates

> By confining the word "call" to people set apart by God for particular ministries we not only imply that there are two levels of Christian, but we encourage those in the "second level" to feel that they can get away with a lower level of dedication and obedience. Once we realize that the fundamental call in the Bible is to follow Jesus Christ as Saviour and Lord, all of us are subject to the same conditions of discipleship, and we all recognize that God has the right to ask us to go anywhere and do anything at any time He chooses."[29]
>
> —*Denis Lane*

Paul's Missionary Vision

The experiences of Paul and his companions recorded in Acts 16:6–14 are often taken as setting a model for a missionary call to cross-cultural missionary work. The urgent call of the man of Macedonia certainly packs a strong appeal to one seeking guidance about whether or not to embark on a missionary vocation. The passage does throw light on the problem, but not perhaps in this strict connection.

Remember that at this time Paul was not a young missionary candidate, but an experienced missionary who had completed one tour of service. So the primary application of this incident would be to an experienced missionary who was waiting on God for direction to his or her next sphere of service, which would be determined by the Lord of the harvest.

Paul's missionary journeys evidenced two things—a combination of careful strategic planning and sensitivity to the Spirit's leading or prohibition. He and his companions had already evangelized in Galatia, and his restless eyes now turned to other unreached areas in Asia. So they "traveled throughout the region of Phrygia and Galatia."

It turned out that his plan was not that of the Holy Spirit, because they were "kept by the Holy Spirit from preaching the word in the province of Asia." Responding obediently to this correction, they journeyed on and "tried to enter Bithynia, but the Spirit of Jesus would not allow them to." The negative authority of the Holy Spirit is as much a part of guidance as His positive thrust.

Were they acting in self-will and out of the will of God? Not for a moment. But the divine Administrator of the missionary enterprise, in exercise of His sovereign will, was directing them, step by step, to the place of His choice— Europe. He achieved His purpose by inward prohibition and the overruling of external circumstances. It was not that Mysia and Bithynia were not in need of the gospel; their time would, and did, come. But first it was Europe.

So Paul and the others did the logical thing. They did not take the prohibition as final and go home. Their commission was to "go and preach," so they pressed on until they could go no further, and reached Troas on the coast. There they waited on God and held a consultation. It was there that the vision followed the previous vetoes.

> During the night Paul had a vision of a man of
> Macedonia standing and begging him, "Come
> over to Macedonia and help us." After Paul had
> seen the vision, we got ready at once to leave for
> Macedonia, *concluding that God had called us* to
> preach the gospel to them.
>
> *Acts 16:9–10* (italics added)

It should be noted that Paul, as leader of the expedition, did not say, "Come on fellows, we are going to Macedonia." He did not act unilaterally, but like the good leader he was, shared his vision with his colleagues and discussed the situation with them. The result was a harmonious decision and willing cooperation. "We got ready . . . concluding that God had called *us* to preach the gospel to them." The word translated "concluding" carries the idea of "putting two and two together." So their joint decision was the action of minds that were guided by the Holy Spirit. There is no mention of how they *felt* about it. The joyous feeling would follow as they obeyed. Once they decided, they lost no time in carrying out the plan.

Similar instances of restraint and redirection have been the experience of many missionaries in succeeding centuries. David Livingstone attempted to go to China, but God redirected him to Africa. Adoniram Judson had India in view as his sphere of service, but the Spirit had chosen Burma. William Carey wanted to serve in Polynesia, but God directed him to India. When we are already in action and need to be directed to the next sphere of service, it is not unreasonable for us to expect somewhat similar (if less dramatic) redirection to the place of God's choice.

Alice Compain, a missionary working with Overseas Missionary Fellowship, had been teaching in a Bible school in Savannakhet, Laos, for a number of years and was on home assignment in England. She was expecting to return to Laos to train church elders who had never been to Bible school, yet were responsible for the teaching and discipling of their own people.

Out of the blue, there came an invitation from the mission to teach in French at the Bible school in Phnom Penh, Cambodia, until she could learn Cambodian. At first she could not see that the Lord had changed her call to Laos, for it seemed that country with its weak army would fall to the Communists before Cambodia. Such a big move to another country with another language seemed like a mountain that she did not have enough faith to remove.

> I could not give an answer to the mission until I was sure that God wanted me there. For about six weeks I vacillated, not knowing clearly what was God's will.
>
> Then in three days the confirmation came. First, friends from Switzerland encouraged me to make the move before I was forty. The next day I travelled to the O.M.F. headquarters in London to attend a day of prayer. The Home Director prayed for those who had been asked to go to Phnom Penh, obviously thinking that we had responded positively, and at the same time the Lord gave me a peace which passes understanding, that it was indeed His will for me, whatever the outcome. The third day I received a letter from the mission director in Thailand, encouraging me that the work in Cambodia was strategic.[30]

She went, and they had an exciting year before Phnom Penh fell. She has been working among Cambodians ever since and has seen much fruit. God has his own way of redirecting His servants to the field of His choice, as He did with Paul.

The Missionary Call

Few subjects in the area of missions have caused more tension and confusion than that of the call to cross-cultural mission. Questions clamor for answer. Can the Great Commission not be fulfilled in the homeland as well as overseas? Is a call biblically necessary? Must it be spectacular or supernatural? Because some missionaries have experienced such a call, is it expected of all who desire to serve?

The crisis that determines the whole future trend of a life is, of course, one of the most crucial any young person is called to face. The question he or she has to answer is, "What is God's will and plan for my life?" The direction of the future will depend on the answer. Our lives are our own to spend, but we can spend them only once. How important it is that we spend them wisely!

> Our wills are ours, we know not how,
> Our wills are ours to make them Thine.
> —*Tennyson*

Every Christian with a spark of ambition desires his or her life to count for God and humankind. Preliminary questions to be settled before the die is cast are whether the sphere of service should be secular or religious and whether it should be in the homeland or overseas. (This last issue is dealt with in the next section.) The many conflicting voices make it difficult to reach a decision, but *it is possible to know the will of God if we are equally willing to embrace either alternative.*

God gave Paul a clear indication of His long-term plan for his life early in his Christian experience, when He said, "Go; I will send you far away to the Gentiles" (Acts 22:21). This meant that the *location* of his service would be on foreign soil, and the *sphere* of his service would not be primarily among his own people but among Gentiles. As he took steps of faith and obedience to the light given, he received light for the next step, and so will we.

It is often said—and by sincere people—"I don't *feel* called to missionary work," as though that disposed of the whole question. But more is involved than mere semantics and emotion. Did Samuel *feel* God's call when he responded, "Speak, for your servant is listening" (1 Samuel 3:10), or did he *hear* it? The call of God is not primarily to the emotions, but to the mind and will. The command remains, whatever our feeling about it.

To hear the *general call* of God to all His disciples to engage in worldwide witness is the first element in a call to service. The geography is secondary. One of the five passages that constitute Christ's Great Commission is unequivocal in its terms: "Therefore go and make disciples of all nations" (Matt. 28:19). This command should lead every Christian to recognize the *general obligation* resting on all believers to engage in witness to Christ somewhere in the world.

The field of operations mapped out for us by the Lord provides plenty of scope for our activities! "You will receive power when the Holy Spirit comes on you; and you will be my witnesses *in Jerusalem, and in all Judea and Samaria, and to the ends of the earth"* (Acts 1:8, italics added).

If we see a man drowning and we ourselves are good swimmers, we do not need special direction to go to his rescue. An inescapable general humane obligation rests on us. How much more so when a person's eternal welfare is at risk?

Two Approaches

There are two ways in which we may approach the question of a potential call to service.

1. We may ask questions such as, *"Where will I find self-fulfillment? Where will my gifts and training find satisfying use? Where will I feel comfortable in my service?"* These are valid questions, but are they central? Do they match the New Testament pattern?

They were not the questions Paul asked. Once he had received the answer to the crucial question, "Who are you, Lord?" (Acts 22:8), and was satisfied that Jesus was indeed the Messiah, his next question was, "What shall I do, Lord?"

He bowed to Christ's sovereignty, arose, and went to Damascus. There he found that God had preceded him and had already communicated a message to Ananias, who in turn passed it on to Paul: "I will show him how much he must suffer for my name" (Acts 9:16). A rather subduing message for a new convert! Paul went forward in glad obedience and without question. The Master had spoken! Self-fulfillment, comfort, and the use of his gifts were matters for the Sovereign Lord to decide—and He could be trusted.

2. The other way to approach the subject is to ask, *"Lord what sphere of service have You prepared for me?"* When James and John tried to preempt the two most prestigious positions in Christ's coming kingdom, He curbed their carnal ambition with ". . . to sit at my right or left is not for me to grant. *These places belong to those for whom they have been prepared"* (Mark 10:40, italics added). The right of appointment to a sphere of service does not lie within our choices, but lies with God. Elsewhere Jesus had said, "You did not choose me, but I *chose you and appointed you* to go and bear fruit" (John 15:16, italics added).

Note the difference in the two approaches. One is horizontal, the other is vertical. The first centers on self—consulting one's own feelings, preferences, and interests. The other approach is to consult God's interests primarily and to choose without reservation the sovereign will of the Lord of the harvest.

When the second course is adopted, the seeker need have no concern about self-fulfillment or the full exploitation of gifts, training, and skills. God's will is good, pleasing, and perfect (Rom. 12:2). That means it cannot be improved upon. God wastes nothing of value.

At Home or Abroad?

Since our Lord's Great Commission can be carried out in the homeland as well as abroad, what are the relative claims and needs of these two spheres of service? There are certain *potentially* eliminating factors, which, while not absolutely ruling out service abroad, should be faced seriously.

1. *Consistently poor health.* Nervous disorders, the need for a restricted diet that may not be available abroad, a tendency to get migraine headaches, or hereditary mental illness—any of these may be an indication that the sphere of service should not be overseas. But now that our home populations are so mixed ethnically, there is no reason why this person should not work among unassimilated ethnic groups at home, and that is frontline missionary work. It is advisable when thinking of missionary work to get a reliable medical opinion before proceeding too far.

2. *Certain temperamental tendencies.* Extremely high-strung or oversensitive people would be borderline candidates for cross-cultural work overseas. In conditions that pertain in most mission fields today, those with a tendency to deep depression or melancholy would not be a helpful addition to the missionary team. Also, those who do not get along well with others in the homeland or who *must* manage other people would probably not wear well on the mission field.

3. *Spiritual unfruitfulness at home* in the present sphere of service. There is little point in going overseas to continue

being ineffective there. A mere change in geography will make no automatic change in a person or his or her service. The potential candidate who has this problem should earnestly seek the conditions of spiritual fruitfulness as shown in Scripture and should comply with those conditions here before seriously contemplating service overseas.

When John R. Mott, who later became the leader of the Student Volunteer Movement, was seriously contemplating whether his service was to be at home or abroad, he fervently sought divine leading. The nearer the time drew to the moment of decision, the more he realized all the implications and his need for more than human guidance. He wrote,

> This matter of choosing a life-field is a very serious question. I thought that everything was settled when I determined to give my life to Christian work, but now looms up a question just as vital—what part of Christian work to enter? . . .
>
> The elements entering into it are so conflicting and complex that I believe *only God* can lead a man to a right decision. I mean to keep myself open and study the whole field, and then just go where God calls."[31]

Bishop Stephen Neill, one of the world's best-informed missiologists, had this to say to a group of ordinands preparing to choose a sphere of service:

> I place on record my conviction that the needs of the mission-field are always far greater than the needs of the church at home; that no human qualifications, however high, render a man or woman more than adequate for missionary work; that there is no other career which affords such scope for enterprise and creative work; and that in

comparison with the slight sacrifice demanded, the reward is great beyond all measure.

Relative Claims

There appears to be no scriptural reason why we should expect a clearer call to service overseas than at home, since the difference is only geographical. We need no special call to spread the gospel; rather we should expect a special call to exempt us from doing so.

It is an undeniable fact that the homelands are more adequately served than the great areas of the unevangelized. In most developed lands there are churches, Bibles, thousands of Christians, Christian literature, and radio and television gospel broadcasts. But in many areas of the world, seeking souls could not find Christ if they wanted to; there is no one to tell them.

It has been said that "facts are the finger of God," and these are indisputable facts. If so, it is a reasonable presumption that if a local community is relatively well served with the gospel, the claims of that community should be secondary to those of the area that is inadequately served. This was one of the lessons Jesus was emphasizing in the parable of the one lost sheep and the ninety-nine safe in the fold.

Paul made two strong statements important to this issue:

> My constant ambition has been to preach the gospel *where the name of Christ was previously unknown.*
> > *Romans 15:20 (Phillips,* italics added).

> I feel myself under a sort of universal obligation. *I owe something to all men,* from cultured Greek to ignorant savage.
> > *Romans 1:14 (Phillips,* italics added)

I have only one candle to burn.
I would rather burn it
where people are in darkness
than in a land flooded with light.

When seeking guidance about missions, one should become literate on the subject. Glean all the information you can. God cannot guide us if we have empty minds. Initial guidance may come to you in your private reading, during a meeting, through a book, through a conversation or sermon, or through some Scripture passage interpreted in its context. Remember that God guides by His Spirit, but the Spirit will never lead contrary to the Word.

Speaking about his own call to China and his missionary experience, J. Hudson Taylor once said, "A missionary who is not clear on this point will at times be at the mercy of the great enemy. When difficulties arise, when in danger of sickness, he or she will be tempted to raise the question which should have been settled before they left the native land."

Is a Special Call Necessary?

For many years it has been the prevalent view in evangelical circles that a special "call" is to be expected if one is to undertake missionary work. This idea has come under challenge, even by some missionary leaders, probably because the call has often been presented in unduly emotional terms and without reference to other equally important factors.

Today, cross-cultural missionary work can be done on the next street. Does this mean that talk of a special call to missionary work abroad is out-of-touch with modern realities? It is possible that in the past too exclusive an emphasis has been attached to such a call. Perhaps the time has come for a reexamination of the subject. Some readily dismiss the concept, but it is the author's conviction that it is not a case of either/or, but of both/and. We need both the acceptance of the call and safeguards against oversubjectivity. While we should be open to fresh light in view of changing world conditions, we should not cavalierly dismiss missionary history.

Reasons other than biblical can be advanced for a clear sense of call from God to the task. In these days of political confusion, spiritual decline, and a frightening renaissance of the occult, the ministry of the Word anywhere is a demanding task. On the mission field, other adverse factors are added: There is the need for mastery of one or two languages if one is to be effective. The climate often is inhospitable. Physical surroundings may be far from ideal, and political conditions may be volatile. To have no clear sense of call from God would leave one open to discouragement and to doubt about whether one is in the right place.

We must also be aware that experience in recent years has proved that chronological age is not always a determinative factor for missionary work. An older person *who is highly motivated* may very well master another language and adapt to an alien culture more successfully than a younger person. Maturity counts, and capacity for growth does not cease at any particular age.

What Is a Call?

There have been many definitions of a call, but one that avoids the danger of oversubjectivity was given by L. T. Lyall: "A call is a conviction that steadily deepens when faced with the facts of the case, so that sooner or later it becomes a matter of obedience or disobedience."

Anyone who seriously studies the missionary activity of the early church will discover that, although the Holy Spirit was installed as the Administrator of the missionary enterprise at Pentecost, He achieved His purpose through human agency. He left the actors with a good deal of initiative in discharging their delegated responsibilities. The divine call was only one element—a very important one—in their guidance. Human factors were prominent, too.

While we must acknowledge that the call of Barnabas and Saul in Acts 13 was exceptional because they were to be initiators of the worldwide missionary enterprise, we should not conclude that there can be or need be no call to those who are less prominent. However, there were many other determinative factors involved in their commission, as well.

They were Spirit-filled men, were biblically literate, were tested in home service, were of proven compatibility, were exercising several spiritual gifts, and were otherwise qualified for cross-cultural work. In addition, they had the enthusiastic confidence of their home church behind them. They did not take the initiative in setting out on their own but waited for the authorizing thrust of the Holy Spirit, and for the church's approval. That is not a bad list of qualifications for cross-cultural missionary work! They did more than "feel called."

No Special Call

It is noteworthy that Paul and Barnabas did not receive a special call for their *second* missionary journey. Paul took the initiative in suggesting a natural follow-up of their first journey (Acts 15:36). The unfortunate dispute over Mark that resulted in the formation of two evangelistic teams was not inspired by the Holy Spirit, but He overruled their failure and carried forward His purpose.

Timothy did not volunteer for missionary service, nor is there a record of his receiving any special call other than his selection by the apostle Paul—under the guidance of the Holy Spirit and with the approval of the church (Acts 16:1–3). On the surface Timothy did not seem an ideal missionary candidate, with his timid nature and indifferent health, but the Spirit gave Paul the spiritual insight to see the potential in the young man. He made a choice that was abundantly justified.

A call does not come by any stereotyped method, nor do the majority of candidates have a spectacular experience. In His sovereignty the Holy Spirit varies His method of guidance with the individual. For this reason, while we can profit from the experience of others, we should not expect or endeavor to duplicate their guidance.

It was persecution that directed Philip to Samaria. Later he was led to the desert road to Gaza by an angelic message. Then he was directed by the Holy Spirit to stay near the chariot of the Ethiopian treasurer. Our last glimpse of him is at Azotus preaching the gospel (Acts 8: 26–31).

As stated elsewhere, God can and sometimes does use a vision or a dream as *one* factor in the indication of His will, but dreams and visions do not exempt us from the use of our own judgment. Faith is content to accept quiet guidance.

In the course of more than sixty-five years of Christian work in the homelands and overseas, I have had many opportunities to prove the Lord in the matter of guidance. I have not always been sensitive and obedient to the Lord's leading, I regret to say. But I can say with truth that there has never been a time when I have sought guidance from the Lord with total willingness to do what He revealed that I have not received clear and satisfying guidance from Him. The problem often has been to bring my will to accept God's will without reservation. But whenever I have capitulated and said, "Lord, I'm willing to be made willing," He has performed the miracle.

I am sure I would never have ventured to accept an important position on the mission field at the age of fifty-two had I not experienced a very clear and definite sense of call. I was home director for the China Inland Mission in Australia, when I received a unanimous invitation from the mission to become its general director. When a previous suggestion had been made, I had vetoed it, for I knew what would be involved and I was unwilling to accept the responsibility. Hundreds of our missionaries were being evacuated from China, and plans were afoot for opening new centers in eight other countries where we had no connections. I felt totally inadequate for the complicated task and was not willing even to entertain the idea.

I was in New Zealand and my wife was in Australia at the time, but we were in close consultation. As I continued praying over the invitation, gradually there came over my spirit the deepening though unwelcome impression that I would have to accept it. A letter from my wife intimated that, as she prayed, the same conviction gripped her heart. She was willing, little as she wanted to take on so much responsibility. This was small comfort.

Staying in the home with me was a close prayer partner of many years. He was a godly man whose counsel I valued very highly. I had shared my problem with him. On the morning he left, he said to me, "As I have been praying about this matter, I believe the Lord has given me a message from Scripture for you. It is 1 Peter 5:1–7. It is a passage about leadership. Verse 7 is, 'Cast all your care upon him for he cares for you.' He is speaking there of the cares of leadership, so if God is calling you to this position, you can cast all your leadership cares on Him."

I went to my room and read the passage in J. B. Phillips's translation, which had just been published. When I came to verse 2, I could hardly believe my eyes. It read,

> "I urge you then to see that your 'flock of God' is
> properly fed and cared for. *Accept the responsi-*

bility of looking after them willingly, and not because you feel you can't get out of it." (italics added)

It diagnosed my position exactly. The mission was my "flock of God," for it had no general director at the time and I was one of the directors in charge. I was unwilling to assume the responsibility, yet felt I would have to do it. I felt inadequate, but the Lord promised help with the burdens of office. It was a passage addressed to leaders and therefore was not taken out of context. It was given to my friend in the place of prayer. I could not help but see that this was God's message to me.

As I changed my attitude from reluctance to glad willingness, the Holy Spirit authenticated the Word to me, and my heart was flooded with the joy and peace of God. As I moved forward in faith, the Lord proved true to His Word.

Another representative case of a special call to cross-cultural mission was that of George K. Harris. In 1947 I had the privilege of traveling with three other missionaries of the Overseas Missionary Fellowship through northwest China and into eastern Tibet, as far as Kumbum. One of my companions was George Harris, a missionary to the Muslims of China. So deep an impression had his ministry made on them, that the hajis—Muslims who had made a pilgrimage to Mecca and were thus holy men—bowed to him as we walked through the streets of Sining.

Years before, at a missionary convention of the Student Volunteer Movement, Dr. Samuel M. Zwemer, apostle to the Muslims, had delivered a burning message on the challenge of the Islamic world:

More Muslims in China than there are in Persia;
More Muslims in China than in all of Egypt.

> More Muslims in China than in the whole of
> Arabia—home and cradle of the Islamic world,
> and no one giving himself to their evangelization!

Among the four thousand students who heard this passionate appeal was William Borden, a young millionaire who afterward prepared to go to China as a missionary to the Muslims. But in Cairo, where he was studying Arabic, he was struck down with cerebrospinal-meningitis and died. On the third anniversary of Borden's death, Dr. Zwemer led a meeting of earnest men and women in the home of Borden's mother. They united in prayer that the Lord would send young men to the Muslims in northwest China, where Borden had planned to go.

George Harris, who was present, tells about his experience on the very same night:

> I was at the prayer meeting of the Great Commission Prayer League. Being in the spirit of prayer, I was conscious of the Lord speaking to me.
>
> "Are you willing to go anywhere for me?"
>
> "Yes, Lord," I replied.
>
> I imagined "anywhere" would be Kano, Nigeria, but to my surprise the Lord flashed across my mind three men from China whom I had met, who had spoken to me about Muslims in northwest China. This fixed my mind on this area of the world, and I rose from my knees convinced that I was to go to China for work among Muslims. As I was coming down the steps a fellow-student said to me:
>
> "Harris, where are you planning to go in the mission field?"
>
> "Just a few minutes ago . . . the Lord called me to the Muslims in China."

As I walked away I heard him mumble: "How odd . . . Muslims in China?"[32]

Harris gave thirty years of his life to the Muslims of China.

An interesting example of a call to the home ministry was that of Selwyn Hughes, whose notes for daily Bible reading have enriched people around the world. Selwyn tells of a memorable sermon he heard just a matter of days prior to his call to the home ministry. He attended a missionary rally in the small town of Crosskeys in England. There he heard a missionary speak on "The Call of God." He based his message on the theme of Mary and the Incarnation and pointed out that, whenever God desires someone to do a special work, he does not leave him to infer it from circumstances alone, but breaks the news personally.

> "God did not allow Mary to infer her high motherhood from the changes that went on in her body" the preacher said, "but broke the news to her beforehand."
>
> I can see him to this day, leaning over the pulpit and shouting into the midst of the congregation. "Before the Incarnation there was an Annunciation! Everyone has a work to do for God in this world, but if God wants you in the ministry or in missionary work, then He will not suffer you to guess, to speculate, to conjecture. He will come and tell you so Himself."

Selwyn went to a night shift in the mine where he worked, and in the silence of the night,

> I heard it. A voice . . . not audible, but speaking directly into my soul: *"I want you in the ministry."* That was all, nothing more. It would be

impossible for me to convey in words the effect those moments had on me. It is as real to me now as it was forty years ago.

Such was the power and impact on my heart that to have asked for a further sign would have been impertinent. God had spoken.[33]

Suggested Procedure for Missionary Candidates

If I were a young Christian contemplating devoting my life to cross-cultural missionary work, I would undertake a procedure something like what follows. This is only suggestive, and each person will need to work out his or her own program, but it covers the main areas involved.

1. I would make sure that my life was fully yielded to Christ's lordship and the control of the Holy Spirit and that I was genuinely willing to do His will, whatever it was. If I had reservations in this area, that would become a subject for earnest prayer.

2. I would obtain a good education, keeping missionary work in mind. One modern language would be included.

3. I would make myself useful in my church and gain some experience in Christian work.

4. I would establish a consistent pattern of devotional life, studying the Bible seriously, especially its missionary thrust.

5. I would be a witness for Christ where I was, engaging in personal evangelism as opportunity arose.

6. I would become literate in the field of mission, taking a special interest in one particular missionary organization even though it might not be the one of my final choice. I would become an intelligent prayer partner.

7. I would give to missions, though my contribution might be small.

8. I would become fully convinced that Christ's Great Commission, compressed into Acts 1:8, lays upon all Chris-

tians the obligation to participate in some way in the missionary enterprise at home or abroad.

9. After inquiry, I would select for my biblical training an evangelical Bible college or seminary with a strong missionary orientation.

10. On completion of my studies, I would try to gain some church experience in a thriving evangelical church.

11. I would be looking to the Lord to lead me to the sphere of service of His choosing and would keep my mind alert to discern His leading. I would expect it to take the form of a growing conviction.

12. I would glean all the information I could about the mission to which I felt drawn, especially in the areas of policy and practice.

13. From the beginning of the process, I would take my pastor into my confidence, because his advice and the encouragement of the church would be invaluable.

14. I would keep in touch with the mission to which I was drawn, by reading their literature, attending a prayer group, and getting to know the personnel.

15. When the hour of final decision arrived, I would set apart a time for prayer and thought. I would lay out the pros and cons of my choices, and ask the Holy Spirit to sway my mind in the direction of His will as I weighed them, and claim the wisdom promised in James 1:5–6.

16. I would make the best judgment I could in the light of the facts, believing that the Lord had answered my prayer for guidance.

17. I would not ask for supernatural or spectacular guidance, but would leave it to Him to give it in the way He sees best.

18. Having made the best decision I could, I would not review it. I would not dig up in unbelief what I had sown in faith. I would expect the Lord, who knows the sincerity of my heart,

to give me heartrest as I moved forward to implementation.

These recommendations may seem unduly complicated, but it should be remembered that they might cover a period of ten years from first interest to arrival on the field. Again, I emphasize that the procedure is only suggestive and may need to be adapted to individual circumstances.

Summary

Decisions concerning vocation are crucial, especially when missionary work is contemplated. Paul's vision in Acts 16 is often taken as an example of an initial missionary call. But Paul was already an experienced missionary at the time. The vision concerned relocation, not an initial call. There the Spirit guided first by restraint and then by constraint. A missionary call is not a feeling but a conviction. The feelings follow the call, but are not always pleasant. Willingness to do God's will anywhere and at any time is a condition precedent to truly seeking guidance—and that condition is not always reached overnight.

Matthew 28:19 is a *general* call and can be fulfilled at home or abroad. But the general must become particular. One's call need not be spectacular and often takes the form of a deepening conviction, through prayer and study of the missionary situation, that God's plan for you is cross-cultural missionary work.

Cross-cultural work can be done on the next street in many cities, but the need for missionaries in vast areas of unevangelized peoples is immeasurably greater than the need in our privileged homelands. Geography is not of prime importance. There are factors that should be considered that potentially eliminate some contemplating overseas missionary work—persistent ill-health, adverse temperamental tendencies, acute depression or mental problems, and spiritual unfruitfulness.

"Facts are the finger of God," and He may give guidance through books, addresses, short-term missionary experience, and many other things. The potential candidate should cultivate a consistent devotional life and should become a missionary intercessor. A clear sense of call is a source of strength in time of danger or testing, but it is only one of several guidelines. If, as you pray, a conviction steadily deepens that God is leading you to missionary work, that is strong evidence of a call.

7. The Hour of Decision

Key Topics:
- The Crunch of Decision
- How to Discern God's Will
- When in Doubt, Wait
- Peace, Guardian of the Heart

> Some of the most precious experiences of one's life may be the times when the Lord seems near, and His Spirit has guided one to act in harmony with the Father's plan. Note carefully that it is faith, the action of the heart in response to the Word, which establishes the requisite relationship to God; the "feeling" of the Spirit's witness afterward is exceedingly precious, but not an essential prerequisite to that action. . . . The impression of God's leading in a missionary call is very precious, but the "feeling" of the call and the actuality of God's plan and guidance must not be equated.[34]
>
> —*E. Stanley Jones*

The Crunch of Decision

After all the preliminary steps have been taken—relevant information gathered, counsel obtained, scriptural principles searched out and weighed, and the whole bathed in prayer—at last the crunch time arrives. We must take the plunge. We must prepare heart and mind for action and thoughtfully come to a decision. While seeking to have "the mind of Christ," we finally have to make up our own minds on the evidence available and then step out in faith.

At this stage it is well to remember that *a great many matters that call for our decision are already taken care of.* The sphere in which we have to decide is not so large as we may think, but it does include some very crucial issues.

Consider these areas, in which it is not prayer for guidance that is required, but simple obedience:

1. *Clear, unequivocal statements of Scriptural principle.* The Bible gives general guidance on all matters of morals, ethics, spiritual life, family life, and church life. The question we have to answer is, *"What does the Bible have to say* in principle or by example on this subject?"

2. *Claims of duty.* This has been treated elsewhere in this book. Relationships impose duties. We have fundamental duties in the areas of family, business, profession, church, and community. There will be minor decisions to make within the scope of particular fundamental duties, and these should be made in the manner suggested in this book. For example, a parent has a fundamental responsibility to provide for his children, but that will involve many minor decisions. The question to answer is, *"Where does my duty lie?"* This will take care of a surprising number of decisions.

3. *Obedience to constituted authority.* Our Lord has told us, "Give to Caesar what is Caesar's, and to God what is God's" (Matt. 22:21). In writing to the Roman Christians, Paul said, "Everyone must submit himself to the governing authorities, for there is no authority except that which God has established. *The authorities that exist have been established by God"* (Rom. 13:1–2, italics added).

This injunction is clear, but there is one more question that calls for an answer when we face decisions: "Does this law or civic responsibility contravene the law of God?" If it does, then our attitude should be the same as that of the apostles: "We must obey God rather than men" (Acts 5:29).

In one hour of decision while he was still a young man, John R. Mott made this observation: "In these days a man cannot afford to make any mistakes. Every decision a man makes shapes his entire life. As I look back on the few years I have been making decisions, I can see how true this is in my case."[35]

Decisions in "Gray" Areas

Before taking the final and irrevocable step, the Christian seeking guidance would be wise to pass the prospective decision through a scriptural sieve. As already pointed out, it is the genius of New Testament Christianity to lay down guiding principles rather than imposing an inflexible set of rules and regulations, as the Pharisees did. God delights in dealing with us as adult persons, not as children under a tutor.

I would suggest seven tests that are of a Scriptural nature. They will help in the resolution of doubtful issues.

1. *Will it bring glory to God?*

This is the paramount test. "Whether you eat or drink or whatever you do, do it all for the glory of God (1 Cor. 10:31). If, as the Westminster Catechism affirms, "the chief end of man is to glorify God and to enjoy Him forever," this should be the primary test of any course of action. If the action would terminate on self and not bring glory to God, that would be sufficient reason to reject it. Our Lord was able to summarize His whole ministry in one verse: "I have brought you glory on earth by completing the work you gave me to do" (John 17:4).

2. *Is it beneficial?*

" 'Everything is permissible,' " said Paul, "but not everything is beneficial" (1 Cor. 10:23). Will it help me to be more Christlike in character and more effective in my witness and service?

3. *Is it constructive?*

" 'Everything is permissible'—but not everything is constructive" (1 Cor. 10:23). Is it for the good of others as well as of myself? Is it calculated to build up Christians in their faith and inspire them to build up others?

4. *Does it have a tendency to enslave one?*

" 'Everything is permissible for me'—but I will not be mastered by anything" (1 Cor. 6:12). Even legitimate things can become tyrannical. They can so demand our time and attention as to cause us to neglect other duties of greater value and importance. For example, it is perfectly legitimate to read good secular literature, but *excessive* secular reading can so enslave the mind that it vitiates the appetite for spiritual literature.

5. *Will it strengthen me against temptation?*

It is futile to pray as our Lord taught us: "Lead us not into temptation but deliver us from evil," if we voluntarily embark on a course that we know will expose us to strong temptation. We are urged to flee from temptations rather than expose ourselves to them.

It is one thing for a uniformed Salvationist to go into a bar to sell her gospel magazine to the patrons, but quite another thing for a young Christian to go to the same bar to "celebrate" with his friends. Any associations that tend to make sin less sinful are to be shunned.

6. *Is it characteristic of the world or of the Father?*

"Do not love the world or anything in the world. If anyone loves the world, the love of the Father is not in him" (1 John 2:15).

There are some relationships, activities, and pleasures that, while not sins, could be termed "hindrances." "Let us throw off everything that hinders" is the exhortation of Hebrews 12:1. We are to throw off everything that would impede our progress in the heavenly race. These things may not necessarily be low and vulgar, but if our participation in them clouds our vision of the ultimate goal, it may be wise to relinquish them.

7. *Could others be affected adversely by my decision?*

In his discussion of the propriety of eating meat that had been offered to idols, Paul gave this guideline to anyone who is serious about his or her influence for God: "If what I eat causes my brother to fall into sin, I will never eat meat again, so that I will not cause him to fall" (1 Cor. 8:13). On another occasion he enunciated another important principle: "Love does no harm to its neighbor" (Rom. 13:10).

The "freedom" of many a moderate drinker has been the undoing of another who did not have the same measure of control of his appetite. If there is any element of doubt, it may be a call to defer further action until, by prayer and diligent searching of the Scriptures, we arrive at a settled conviction of the correct course to follow.

On the other hand, it may be that we have a "weak" conscience on the matter under review, which needs to be educated by further light from the Word. It is quite possible that, through bondage to tradition or prejudice, we may have doubts about what Scripture does not condemn.

In this exercise we must be careful not to overlook the gracious ministry of the Holy Spirit, whose work it is to guide us into all truth. "The leadership and discipline of the Holy Spirit through the moral standards of the Word—this is the basis of all moral living."

It is both interesting and profitable to follow the varying ways in which God guides His servants into the path He has chosen for them and assists them in their decision-making, while not robbing them of their freedom of choice. One appropriate illustration of this process concerns the development of a college for training young Christian leaders for the emerging churches of Melanesia. The project was conceived by several mission leaders. In their search for a man to lead the college, which was to be based in Papua New Guinea, the initiators were directed to Gilbert J. McArthur. He had been manager of a country airline in Australia, had trained as a Baptist minister, and had had missionary experience in Papua New Guinea.

God had created in Gilbert's heart a more than passing interest in the Christian Leaders' Training College, as it was to be called, and he offered to stimulate prayer interest in the project in his home area. Before long it became clear that it was God's will for him to be involved in more than a prayer ministry. A tentative approach was made by the committee to determine if he would consider an invitation to become principal of the college.

The situation was complicated for him because he was pastor of a church, and he was also presented with two other strategic opportunities at the same time, one of which was in Indonesia. This was a *complex* decision that he faced, for only one of these could be the Lord's plan.

"All these valid claims," he wrote, "cause us to be continually before the Lord for a clear discernment of His purpose for us. My wife and I would now readily recognize that the field and its needs have first claim upon us, and would willingly respond to His clear direction."

His background experience had been extensive—airline management, theological and linguistic training, anthropology and allied studies, as well as pastoral ministry. When the "sediment" had settled, the divine plan gradually became clear, and he wrote to the secretary: "For myself personally, I must confess that I feel more equipped for the work of the college. There have been some quite strong indications in this regard. My own deacons to a man feel they and the church could readily thrust me out into such a work. . . . All I can say is that I am aware of a strong sense of compulsion to be found in the most effective place of service." So his appointment was confirmed.

The subsequent success of the college in training hundreds of men and women now holding important posts in the churches of Papua New Guinea owes a great debt to the herculean labors and spiritual leadership of Gilbert McArthur.[36]

If this story is analyzed, it will be seen that it illustrates many of the guidance principles we have been considering.

How to Discern God's Will

There are different types of decisions with which we are faced in the guidance process, and each requires individual treatment. They fall into several categories.

1. *Personal decisions* that affect lifestyle or vocation—marriage, occupation, education, church memberships, and so on.

2. *Straightforward decisions,* where a single moral principle would be applicable, for example, something that involves dishonesty. Such decisions call for obedience rather than prayer.

3. *Non-moral decisions,* decisions in which no moral issues are involved.

4. *Complex decisions* in which more than one issue is involved. Three of the most complicated subjects prominent in the public mind today are war, abortion, and divorce. Each of these involves several moral issues, and therefore demands an unusually sensitive balancing of the alternatives. But for this, heavenly wisdom is available (James 1:5).

5. *Indeterminate matters.* These have been referred to in the

previous section, but it should be pointed out that there are non-moral issues concerning which the Bible makes no pronouncement but leaves some liberty of choice, as in the case of eating meat offered to idols. Paul did not prohibit all eating of such meat, but left it to the individual judgment of mature believers, who, to use Paul's statement, "know that an idol is nothing at all in the world." However, we must ensure that our freedom should not cause others to stumble. In these *gray areas,* the following attitude would be advisable.

(a) If you experience serious reservations and uncertainty, that is a call to review the situation.

The scriptural position is, "Blessed is the man who does not condemn himself by what he approves. But the man who has doubts is condemned if he eats, because his eating is not from faith; and everything that does not come from faith is sin" (Rom. 14:22–23).

(b) If your decision would create problems of conscience for others not so strong in the faith, give them the benefit of the doubt (1 Cor. 10:23–24).

In the previous chapter there is a suggested procedure for those contemplating missionary work. By revising that procedure somewhat, a series of suggestions can be compiled for those who face other than missionary decisions that are not resolved by clear statements of Scripture, clear call of duty, or demands of constituted authority that do not contravene God's commands:

1. Be unconditionally willing to do it, whatever it is. It may be that your will needs to be redirected. Be willing to be made willing.

2. Be obedient to any light the Lord has already given. If you are not obeying that, why expect more?

3. Be patient. The road ahead may not be revealed all at once; it seldom is. But God will show you each step as you need to

take it. We sing the hymn "One Step Enough for Me," but don't always mean it.

4. Remember the intellectual component in this exercise. John Wesley maintained, "God generally guides me by presenting *reasons to my mind* for acting in a certain way"— *not* feelings to my heart.

5. Gather all the information you can about the options that are open to you.

6. Seek advice from your Christian parents, your pastor, or a trusted Christian counselor. However, don't allow them to make the decision for you. It is your life that is at stake, and you will have to live with the consequences of that decision.

7. Ensure that the course you propose to pursue is biblically legitimate. Submit it to the test of Scripture.

8. List the pros and cons of the course you propose, and as you weigh them, ask the Holy Spirit to sway your mind in the direction of His will, believing that He does it in keeping with James 1:5.

9. Don't ask for extraordinary guidance, for that is the exception and not the rule, especially as you mature spiritually. Spectacular signs are given only by the sovereign choice of God. Faith is content with quiet guidance.

10. Make the best decision you can in the light of the facts, believing God has answered your prayer for wisdom.

11. Expect the witness of the Spirit in a deepening conviction that this is the will of God for you. Circumstances may confirm your guidance.

12. Be prepared for Satan to challenge your decision. He did that with the Master.

13. Unless action is urgent, allow a little time to elapse, and if the conviction remains and the peace of God guards your heart, act with confidence.

14. Don't dig up in unbelief what you have sown in faith.

When in Doubt, Wait

A story is told of Phillips Brooks, the great Boston preacher. A friend who came to visit him was ushered into the preacher's study. On entering, he found his host pacing up and down, evidently in great agitation.

"What's the matter, Phillips?" his friend asked.

"Matter enough! I'm in a hurry and God's not!"

Most of us will have no difficulty in identifying with Dr. Brooks. But it is when we are in that state that we are in danger of taking precipitate and premature action that we may have reason to regret later.

On one occasion in my youth, I was praying for guidance on a matter that was very important to me. In my impatience I was strongly tempted to act before I was sure of the Lord's will. My father gave me some advice then that has proved valuable, based on his own experience.

He had lost his job during the worldwide depression. Weeks went by without any employment opening up. With a family to support, he was naturally anxious to do something. Pressure was brought to bear on him to purchase a small business. He prayed about it, but was inwardly uneasy about taking the step. However, although unsure, he felt he could wait no longer. Impetuously, he signed the contract—as a result of which he eventually sustained a considerable financial loss. The very next morning he received the offer of an excellent position as accountant for a large firm. He accepted it but was burdened with a business that was not successful. "If only I had waited!" he said.

"When you are seeking guidance," he told me, "there are three words that are important. The first is *wait!* The second is *wait!* The third is *wait!* The important lesson is, "Don't allow anyone to pressure you into action when you are not sure." Of course the time comes when we must take action.

But a safe maxim is "whenever there is doubt, wait."

In a recent letter, a missionary executive wrote,

> The temptation here is to think that if we make plans well enough, we are masters of our own fate. Soon enough God will show us that our best-made plans, made without Him, will crumble and collapse, or worse still, come to fruition without blessing.
>
> Often eager planners like myself have to wait. God's delays might have wonderful unseen factors that make the fulfillment all the more wonderful and complete. Often the very process of delay and disappointment help us to sift our motives and turn our eyes to the Lord in a way they were not when we first formulated our plans.

Dr. Henry W. Frost, then Canadian director of the China Inland Mission, was facing an important and seemingly urgent decision. He was engaged in studying the Bible with this in mind. "As I meditated on the verses, it did not take me long to decide which was the harder. Waiting on the Lord is comparatively easy; waiting *for* the Lord is decidedly hard. Just now it was a case of waiting *for* Him, and I fear I did not make much of a success of it." Many of us can identify with him in that regard.

Although God is never in a hurry, He is never late. His timing is perfect, because He has control of all that happens. This is a difficult lesson for us impatient mortals to learn. However, it must be mastered if we are to keep in step with God. It is when we are under pressure to make a decision that we are most vulnerable and liable to make a serious mistake. We need the restraint of the Holy Spirit as well as His constraint, but we are less likely to be sensitive to His prohibitions. We must be as willing for our Guide to say no to our plans as yes.

Wait! for the day is breaking,
  Though the dull night be long,
Wait! God is not forsaking
  Thy heart, Be strong—Be strong!
Wait! 'tis the key to pleasure
  And to the peace of God;
O tarry thou His leisure—
  Thy soul shall bear no load.

C. Townsend

Should God veto a certain course of action on which your heart is set, be assured that He has not done it out of caprice. It is because of His deep concern that you do not miss the best He has for you. It is the expression of His perfect wisdom and love. "God disciplines us *for our good,* that we may share in his holiness" (Heb. 12:10, italics added). It is the highest wisdom to wait for the gradual unfolding of God's will in providence.

Sometimes when our cherished plans are checkmated, it is not denial, only delay for some wise purpose. The experience of the Israelites immediately after their deliverance from Egypt is a case in point. From the place where they crossed the Red Sea to the borders of Canaan at Kadesh Barnea, the journey would normally take only eleven days (Deut. 1:2). The way they traveled, however, it took them several months.

It must be remembered that the Israelites had lived as slaves all their lives; others made the decisions for them. So God in His compassion allowed them sufficient time to adjust to their new status. His reasoning is given in Exodus 13:17–18.

> When Pharaoh let the people go, God did not lead them on the road through the Philistine country, though that was shorter. For God said, "If they

face war, they might change their minds and
return to Egypt." So God led the people around by
the desert road toward the Red Sea.

The wisdom of this detour soon became apparent. When
they began to meet opposition and the going became difficult,
they soon showed how ill-prepared they were for the conflict
and hardships that lay ahead. They desperately needed the
brief but gentle initiation of the desert experience to toughen
and mature them and fit them for conflict against war-
experienced foes.

So does God at times lead his servants on what seems like
a pointless detour. His leading crosses our desires and
inclinations, because He is working for eternity and has
deeper purposes in view.

After his dramatic conversion, John Newton was very
zealous and wanted to make rapid growth in his Christian life.
But he did not recognize the answer to his prayers when it
came, and we sometimes find ourselves in the same situation.
Here are three stanzas of his poem in which he tells his
experience.

> I asked the Lord that I may grow
> In faith and love and every grace,
> Might more of His salvation know
> And seek more earnestly His face.
>
> I thought that in some favoured hour
> At once He'd answer my request,
> And by His love's constraining power
> Subdue my sins, and give me rest.
>
> Instead of that He made me feel
> The hidden evils of my heart,
> And bade the angry powers of hell
> Assault my soul in every part.

Discovering His Will For Your Life • **143**

But this puzzling experience led Newton out into undreamed of blessing and usefulness.

So, by the disciplines of the desert road, God kept His people dependent on Him, while at the same time developing their characters. Often it is only after some "detour" experience that we discern the gracious purpose the Lord had in view all along. (See John 13:7.)

Peace, Guardian of the Heart

One of the time-honored proof texts used in connection with guidance is Colossians 3:15.

> Let the peace of Christ rule in your hearts, since as members of one body you were called to peace. (NIV)
> Let the ruling principle in your hearts be God's peace. (Rotherham)
> Let Christ's peace be the arbiter in your hearts. (NEB)

The usual interpretation of this text is that the believer seeking guidance should regard the presence or absence of the peace of Christ in the heart as and after a decision is made, as either a confirmation or a condemnation of that decision.

In support of that position, it is advanced that the word *rule* is often used in the original language to refer to the official or referee judging at the Olympic Games. So, when one is moving in the direction of the will of God, one can expect the Holy Spirit to fill the office of referee or umpire in the situation by imparting Christ's peace to one's heart. Where that is absent, the decision apparently was not God's will or the time was not ripe, and the matter should therefore be reviewed.

Contrary to this view, it is plausibly argued that the context of the verse does not deal with decision-making, but with the love, peace, and unity that should be characteristic of believers. Consequently, the application is not relevant to decision-making. And in any case, there may be other causes for the absence of peace.

It is true that the presence of unrest and disquiet might be traceable to other sources than God's displeasure. Further, this test is very subjective and, therefore, has its perils and weaknesses. But the concept that God confirms or vetoes our decisions by imparting or withholding peace does not rest on Colossians 3:15 alone. Paul exhorted the Philippian Christians:

> Do not be anxious about anything, but in
> everything, by prayer and petition, with
> thanksgiving, present your requests to God.
> And the peace of God, which transcends all
> understanding, will guard your hearts and
> your minds in Christ Jesus.
>
> *Philippians 4:6–7*

These verses are sometimes misconstrued as a subjective guide to decision-making. But Paul is not speaking here of an inner sense of peace as God's reassurance to those who are moving in His will in their decisions. The context deals with not being anxious but being prayerful about everything, and the result will be the enjoyment of peace.

But need the passage be limited to that sole context? *Is not Paul stating a general principle?* Rotherham translates the verse, "Let the *ruling principle* in your hearts be God's peace" (italics added). In expounding the same verse, Curtis Vaughan said, "Perhaps we should not limit the word, but should understand it as including peace in the largest sense."

Is it not true—leaving the controversial verses out of consideration—that when we are walking in the Spirit and in communion with God, doing His will as far as we know it, we do experience the peace of God which passes all understanding? There is a good case for the contention that the peace of God can be expected when one's decision is in line with God's will. J. I. Packer affirms this when he writes, "Cherish the divine peace that Paul says garrisons (guards, keeps safe and steady) the hearts of those who are in God's will."

The late Arthur Wallis tells of one of his experiences of guidance:

> In 1962 I received my first invitation to minister overseas. New Zealand was to prove a watershed in my ministry. At first I turned the invitation down, as I could see no way that I could be away for long enough to warrant travelling so far.
>
> But the young men in New Zealand who had invited me, would not take "no" for an answer. They wrote again and said that they had prayed and fasted, and were assured that I was the man, and had accordingly paid my round trip fare to New Zealand!
>
> "What impertinence!" I thought. "If God has revealed it to them, why has He not revealed it to me?" I went through a time of confusion, until in desperation I flung the whole issue at God's feet telling Him that I didn't care whether I went or not. *Immediately I came into peace,* and then heard the word, "Go, and I will be with your mouth and teach you what you shall speak."[37]

He subsequently went to New Zealand for three months of fruitful ministry, stayed two years, and had more openings than he could entertain.

Is it not true, conversely, that, when in our decisions we move out of the will of God, the dove of peace departs? This would be equally true if the above passages from Philippians and Colossians were not in the Bible. Of course it is taken for granted that if there are genuine disturbers of the peace in our lives they must be faced and dealt with honestly.

Nor should it be forgotten that there is such a thing as a "false peace." " 'Peace, peace,' they say, when there is no peace" (Jer. 8:11). Jonah experienced a false peace and was able to sleep through the storm although pursuing a rebellious course!

Waiting to implement a decision for a brief period after arriving at it is a wise procedure, when it is not urgent. That allows the Lord the opportunity to veto, restrain, or confirm the decision. He will not be displeased because a believer is sensitive to His approval or disapproval.

The enjoyment of the peace of Christ when taking the next step in acting on a decision springs from our knowledge of God and communion with Him, rather than from a correct formula of guidance. When we move in the will of God, both mind and heart will be at peace, even when we meet lions in the way.

> Let Him lead thee blindfold onwards,
> Love needs not to know;
> Children whom the Father leadeth
> Ask not where they go.
> Though the path be all unknown
> O'er moors and mountains lone.
>
> Give no ear to reason's questions,
> Let the blind man hold
> That the sun is but a fable
> Men believed of old.
> At the breast the babe will grow,
> Whence the milk he need not know.
>
> *—Gerhard Tersteegen*

Summary

Some decisions are straightforward and some complex, and each will require a slightly different procedure. There are moral and non-moral decisions, and there are gray areas in which the issues are mixed. In these indeterminate areas, if one has serious reservations, especially if the decision could cause conscience problems to others, review of the issues is called for.

Obedience to light already given opens the way to the next step. We should trust God to give the wisdom promised in James 1:5 as we come to the point of decision. Information should have been gathered and advice sought. We should have confirmed the biblical legitimacy of our options. Then pros and cons should have been listed, and we should have trusted the Holy Spirit to sway our minds in the direction of God's will. The final step is to make the best decision in the light of all the facts. Unless the decision is urgent, a little time should be allowed to elapse. If the conviction remains and the peace of God guards our hearts, then we should act with confidence.

There are general areas where further guidance is unnecessary—clear, unequivocal statements of Scripture; the claims of duty; and obedience to constituted authority when it does not contravene the law of God. Within these general areas, minor, specific guidance may be needed. Answering the following questions might help clarify gray areas: Is it for God's glory? Is it beneficial and constructive? Does it strengthen against temptation, or does it tend to enslave? When in doubt, wait! Don't allow others to pressure you into premature action.

"Let the ruling principle in your hearts be God's peace."

8. Walking in Wisdom

Key topic:
• Cautions about Guidance

Cautions about Guidance

Scattered throughout the Scriptures are thousands of "very great and precious promises" (2 Peter 1:4), promises to match every conceivable situation we are likely to face. In the previous generation, many Christians used to have "promise boxes," which held little rolls of paper with biblical promises printed on them. It was a common mealtime practice in many Christian homes to pass the box around the table. Each would take a promise and read it, sharing its message—a message of comfort and encouragement. In this way members of the family became familiar with the great promises of the Bible.

But Scripture is not all promises! There are many *commands and warnings* as well. They form an integral component of the Word of God. Yet, I have never seen a "command box" or a "warning box." This casts light on our natural mindset. We would rather appropriate a promise than obey a command or heed a warning.

In view of this fact and the complexity of the subject of guidance, it may be appropriate to conclude this book by recapitulating some of the cautions that are stated or are implicit in the preceding chapters. It is my hope that a thoughtful reading of them before closing the book will be profitable.
1. Beware of paying more attention to the mechanics of guidance than to the leading of the Guide and of being more concerned about matters such as geographical location than about holy living.

2. Avoid the mistake of equating God's permission with His direct will, as Balaam did.

3. Don't allow troubles or hindrances to be a decisive factor. Early in Paul's Christian experience, God said of him, "I will show him how much he must suffer for my name" (Acts 9:16). Knowing this did not deter Paul from obeying his commission. Nor did he allow subsequent afflictions to deflect him (Acts 16:22–24).

4. Do not take an *unsupported* answer to prayer as an expression of God's will. When the Israelites complained that they had no meat to eat, nothing but "this manna"—the psalmist records that the Lord "gave them what they asked for, but sent a wasting disease upon them" (Ps. 106:15). Sometimes God can teach us important spiritual lessons only by letting us have our own way.

5. Do not consider mere external need to be sufficient guidance. It is a factor, but only one. After we have done our utmost, there will still be vast unmet needs in the world. We should test our guidance in other ways as well.

6. Be alert to the possibility of mistaking the voice of God.

7. Never take guidance from one text of Scripture when the whole spirit of Scripture is to the contrary. Note how adroitly Jesus evaded this peril when tempted by the devil in the desert.

8. Do not rest on the mere letter of the Word, for "the letter kills, but the Spirit gives life" (2 Cor. 3:6). The Pharisees adhered fanatically to the letter of the Word, but by their actions denied its spirit. It was this attitude that drew strong censure from the Lord.

9. Beware of guidance that presses one to act when not sure. See 1 Samuel 13:12–14, where it is recorded that Saul "felt compelled to offer the burnt offering," thus intruding into the office reserved for priests. With what result? "You acted foolishly. . . . your kingdom will not endure."

10. Should you be out of touch with the Lord—as Jonah was—check out carefully any seemingly favorable providential circumstance. Jonah found a ship all ready to sail!

11. Shun professed guidance that is based on superstition or the forbidden arts—astrology, fortune telling, ouija boards, tarot cards, mediums. The Scriptures are clear on this point:

> Let no one be found among you who . . . practices
> divination or sorcery, interprets omens, engages
> in witchcraft, or casts spells, or who is a medium
> or spiritist, or who consults the dead. Anyone who
> does these things is detestable to the Lord.
>
> *Deuteronomy 18:10–12*

> Saul died because he was unfaithful to the Lord;
> he did not keep the word of the Lord, and even
> consulted a medium for guidance, and did not
> enquire of the Lord.
>
> *1 Chronicles 10:13–14*

12. Don't resort to "casting lots" as a means of determining the divine will. It is a very old practice, and was used in Israel, "but only in the choice of a successor to Judas (Acts 1:26) is the use of lots by Christ's followers mentioned. As a distinctly Jewish mode of seeking divine direction, its use was appropriate for the occasion. With the coming of the Spirit at Pentecost to take direction of the affairs of the Church, its use is never mentioned again."[38] Remember that Satan and the Lord both have an even chance! God has given us minds and expects us to use them.

13. Don't pursue any path when there is an inward block or restraint of the Holy Spirit. He guides us by restraint as well as constraint. Paul had this experience:

> Paul and his companions traveled throughout the
> region of Phrygia and Galatia, having been kept

by the Holy Spirit from preaching the word in the province of Asia. "When they came to the border of Mysia, they tried to enter Bithynia, but the Spirit of Jesus would not allow them to.

Acts 16:6–7

14. The Lord does not make us infallible and mistake-proof. Therefore, while not doubting our leading, we should remain open to further light. Sometimes a mistake casts further light on our problem.

15. Be suspicious of any purported leading that would help us to sidestep a difficult choice that has the appearance of the will of God.

> Thy way, not mine O Lord,
> However dark it be,
> Lead me by Thine own hand;
> Choose out the path for me.
>
> Smooth let it be, or rough,
> It will be still the best;
> Winding or straight, it leads
> Right onwards to Thy rest.
>
> I dare not choose my lot,
> I would not if I might;
> Choose Thou for me my God,
> So shall I walk aright.
>
> *—Horatius Bonar*

Epilogue

In the preceding pages the subject of guidance has been viewed from many angles. It is a component of the Christian life that has often been confusing to both young and old. It is the author's hope that some light has been shed from the Scriptures on the path of some who are seeking guidance.

I have sought to distinguish between things that differ, to balance positive and negative aspects of the issue, to explain some problem Scriptures, and to suggest procedures that seem to have biblical support. In treating a theme on which so many conflicting views are entertained, one can express one's views only with humility and without undue dogmatism. But I can say with truth that I have proved the validity of my views. It is for the reader to test them alongside the Scriptures and in experience.

Is it not a cause for adoring wonder that the Sovereign God who controls the movements of untold myriads of heavenly bodies pauses to involve Himself in our little concerns, that He has assured saints of succeeding generations that He would be their Guide? No other religion has a god who promises, "I will counsel you with my eye upon you"! (Ps. 32:8 RSV). The Muslim knows no such hope. To him, whatever happens is "the will of Allah," to be received with fatalistic resignation.

How different for the Christian who embraces the privilege of having the eternal God for ever and ever; "he will be our guide even to the end" (Ps. 48:14). Let us do Him the honor of availing ourselves of the unique privilege that is ours, with praise and thanksgiving.

Notes

1. Arthur I. Davidson, *High Adventure with God* (Manila: Living Books, 1974), 14–15.

2. S. Pearce Carey, *William Carey* (London: Hodder & Stoughton, 1924), 289–90.

3. E. Stanley Jones, *Christian Maturity* (Nashville: Abingdon, 1957).

4. A. W. Tozer, *The Knowledge of the Holy* (Harrisburg, Penn.: Christian Publications, 1961), 10.

5. S. Pearce Carey, *William Carey,* 125.

6. J. I. Packer, *Laid Back Religion* (London: InterVarsity Press, 1989), 75.

7. A. Morgan Derham, *The Mature Christian* (London: Marshall, Morgan, & Scott, 1961), 74.

8. Francis Foulkes, *The Epistle to the Ephesians* (London: Tyndale Press, 1963), 77.

9. H. C. G. Moule, *Ephesians* (London: Cambridge University Press, 1910), 74.

10. J. R. W. Stott, *Favourite Psalms* (Chicago: Moody Press, 1988), 44.

11. Gary Friesen, *Decision-making and the Will of God* (Portland, Ore.: Multnomah Press, 1980), 100.

12. L. S. Chafer, *He That Is Spiritual* (London: Marshalls, 1929), 113.

13. Clarence W. Hall, *Samuel Logan Brengle* (London: Salvation Army, 1976), 157–158.

14. M. Blaine Smith, *Knowing God's Will* (Downers Grove, Ill.: InterVarsity Press, 1979), 30.

15. Marvin Rickard, *Let it Grow!* (Portland, Ore.: Multnomah Press, 1984), 16–19.

16. John White, *The Fight* (Downers Grove, Ill.: InterVarsity Press, 1979), 151.

17. J. F. Walvoord, *The Holy Spirit* (Grand Rapids, Mich.: Dunham Publishers, 1954), 221.

18. C. S. Lewis, *The World's Last Night* (New York: Harcourt Brace Jovanovich, 1959), 9.

19. Basil Matthews, *John R. Mott* (London: Hodder & Stoughton).

20. Kenneth L. Pike, pamphlet.

21. Robert E. Speer, *The Principles of Jesus* (New York: Association Press, 1902), 34.

22. Oliver R. Barclay, *Guidance* (Downers Grove, Ill.: InterVarsity Press, 1976), 157.

23. Robert E. Speer, *Seeking the Mind of Christ* (New York: Revell, 1926), 61.

24. Tim LaHaye, *Finding the Will of God* (Grand Rapids, Mich.: Zondervan, 1989), 128 ff.

25. L. S. Chafer, *He That Is Spiritual,* 115.

26. J. C. McCauley, *Acts of the Apostles* (Grand Rapids, Mich.: Eerdmans, 1946), 179.

27. Ibid.

28. Edward England, *My Call to Preach* (London: Highland Books, 1986), 25.

29. Denis Lane, *When God Guides* (Singapore: O.M.F. Books, 1984), 4.

30. Denis Lane, Ibid. 63, 113.

31. Basil Matthews, *John R. Mott*, 78.

32. M. R. Bradshaw, *Torch for Islam* (London: O.M.F. Books, 1965), 27.

33. Edward England, *My Call to Preach,* 83.

34. E. Stanley Jones, *Christian Maturity,* 00.

35. Basil Matthews, *John R. Mott,* 179.

36. J. O. Sanders, *Planting Men in Melanesia,* (Mt. Hagen: C.L.T. College, 1978), 30–31.

37. Edward England, *My Call to Preach,* 104.

38. D. E. Hiebert, *Zondervan Bible Dictionary* (Grand Rapids, Mich.: Zondervan, 1989), 128.

Note to the Reader

The publisher invites you to share your response
to the message of this book by writing Discovery House
Publishers, P. O. Box 3566, Grand Rapids, MI 49501,
U.S.A. or by calling 1-800-283-8333. For information
about other Discovery House publications, contact us at
the same address and phone number.